Peter Boge

Algorithmic Quantum Esotericism

Peter Boge

Algorithmic Quantum Esotericism

Decoding the invisible forces that direct global financial flows

Non-fiction

Legal Notice

Bibliographic Information from the German National Library: The German National Library lists this publication in the German National Bibliography; detailed bibliographic data is available online at http://dnb.dnb.de.

Publisher: BoD · Books on Demand GmbH, Überseering 33, 22297 Hamburg, bod@bod.de

Patreon: https://www.patreon.com/cw/authorpeterboge
Substack: https://substack.com/@peterboge
Author homepage: https://peter.boge.com.gt/author/

Print: Libri Plureos GmbH, Friedensallee 273, 22763 Hamburg

ISBN: 978-3-6963-5609-5

FSC www.fsc.org
MIX
Papier aus verantwortungsvollen Quellen
Paper from responsible sources
FSC® C105338

Table of Contents

PROLOGUE – THE INVISIBLE FORCES

Decoding Algorithmic Esotericism
From the temple priests of Mesopotamia to the quantum algorithms of financial markets

"The most powerful forces of an era are often those that hardly anyone sees."

The Sound of Invisibility

There is no bell toll to announce the beginning of a new world.
No fanfares.
No revolution in the streets.

The greatest upheavals of history usually happen in silence.
The Roman Empire did not fall in a single day.
The feudal system did not disappear overnight.
The Industrial Revolution did not begin with an official declaration.
And the digital revolution was not proclaimed either.
It just happened.
While most people continued living their everyday lives.

Today, we are experiencing another such transition.

But this time, it does not only affect our tools.
It affects the very structure of reality itself.

The New Invisibility

Modern humans live in a world shaped by decisions they never see.

When a flight ticket suddenly becomes more expensive.
When a loan is approved or denied.
When a stock rises.
When a post appears on a social network.
When billions in capital leave a continent.

Behind these events, there is increasingly rarely a human being.
Between cause and effect, there is increasingly an algorithm today.
Not as a tool.
But as an independent instance of decision-making.

This is the true revolution of our time.
Not digitalization.
Not the internet.
Not artificial intelligence.
But the shifting of decision-making power.

From Visible to Invisible Power

Historically, power was recognizable.
The king wore a crown.
The general led an army.
The priest spoke before a congregation.
The factory owner owned his machines.

Power had a face.
You could see it.
You could fight it.
You could overthrow it.

But the power of the 21st century often no longer has a body.
It exists as:

- a mathematical model
- an optimization function
- a neural network
- a trading algorithm
- a data infrastructure

The new power is not hidden because it is secret.
It is hidden because it has become too complex.

The Birth of Algorithmic Esotericism

The word "esotericism" comes from Greek.
Originally, it referred to knowledge for an inner circle.
Knowledge that was not meant for everyone.

Modern society considers itself the opposite.
We believe in:

- transparency
- science
- public access
- enlightenment

Yet paradoxically, this very development creates new forms of esotericism.
Not through secrecy.
But through complexity.

Most people do not understand:

- money creation
- derivatives
- high-frequency trading
- neural networks
- cryptography
- quantum computing

Not because these systems are secret.
But because their complexity exceeds the limits of human intuition.

Thus, a new form of hidden knowledge emerges.
An algorithmic esotericism.

The Financial Markets as the Vanguard of the Future

Nowhere is this development more evident than in the global financial markets.
Financial markets have always been laboratories of power.
Innovations were tested here long before they reached society:

- double-entry bookkeeping
- insurance
- central banks
- global communication
- computerization

Today, the markets are once again serving as a testing ground.
This time, for machines.
Already, a significant portion of trading volume is no longer triggered by humans.
Rather, by systems.

These systems analyze:

- news streams
- satellite data

- weather data
- supply chains
- social media
- geopolitical events

and react within timeframes that human perception can no longer grasp.
The human observes.
The machine acts.

The Transition from Thinking to Calculation

This is where the true turning point lies.
Earlier generations assumed that decisions arise from thinking.
A human analyzes.
A human judges.
A human decides.

But modern systems follow a different logic.
They do not understand.
They calculate.
And yet they often achieve better results.

This challenges one of the deepest assumptions of modernity:
The notion that understanding is a prerequisite for action.
Machines act successfully without understanding.

Humans often understand without acting successfully.
Between the two, a growing disparity in power emerges.

The Quantum Paradigm

The next stage of development may already be on the horizon.
The term "quantum trading" is often misunderstood.
It is not primarily about exotic computers.
It is about a new way of thinking.

The classical world asks:
Which solution is the correct one?
The quantum world asks:
Which possibilities exist simultaneously?

While traditional systems search for answers, quantum systems search through entire landscapes of possible futures.
The significance of this change can hardly be overstated.
Because whoever can analyze many possible futures at once gains an advantage over those who consider only one future.
Thus, power becomes the ability to master probability spaces.

The New Aristocracy

Every era produces its own elites.
In the Middle Ages, it was the nobility.
In the Industrial Age, the factory owners.
In the Financial Age, the bankers.

In the algorithmic age, new centers of power are emerging.
Not necessarily visible.
Not necessarily democratically legitimized.
But of enormous reach.

The decisive resource is now:
Prediction.

Whoever can predict behavior—

- markets,
- consumers,
- voters,
- states—

gains structural power.
Not through coercion.
But through anticipation.

The New Financial Metaphysics

At this point, technology touches philosophy.
Because modern markets are developing properties once attributed to religious systems.
They appear:

- omnipresent
- invisible
- complex
- impersonal

They reward and punish. They create wealth and crises. They influence billions of people.
Yet no one controls them completely.

This recalls an ancient human experience:
The encounter with forces that seem greater than the individual.
In the past, they were called gods. Today, they are called markets.
Tomorrow, perhaps algorithms.

The Real Question

This book is not about computers.
Not about artificial intelligence. Not even primarily about financial markets.
It is about power.

About the oldest question of civilization:
Who decides?

And a new question:
What happens when those who decide are no longer human?

Perhaps we are not experiencing a technological revolution.
Perhaps we are witnessing the emergence of a new form of rule.
Not through violence.
Not through ideology.
Not through religion.
But through calculation.

The View Behind the Curtain

The following chapters are a journey.
From the temples of Mesopotamia to the data centers of the present.
From the priests of antiquity to the architects of artificial intelligence.
From the first bookkeepers to the developers of quantum-inspired models.

It is the story of a continuous search for predictability.
For control.

For order.
And thus, the story of power itself.

Because the real question is not:
Can algorithms change the world?
But rather:
Have they already begun to do so – while we are still trying to understand what is even happening?

The answer to this question may determine the political, economic, and cultural shape of the 21st century.

And this is precisely where our investigation begins.

PART I – THE BIRTH OF INVISIBILITY

Chapter 1 – The Invention of Hidden Order

How Rule Emerged from Information

"The first great revolution of humanity was not agriculture. It was the administration of agriculture."

The Error of Visible Power

When people think about the origins of power, they often imagine weapons.
They think of:

- kings
- armies
- conquests
- walls
- palaces

But this notion falls short. Violence can establish rule, but it cannot organize it permanently.
No king can supervise every farmer. No army can control every harvest. No ruler can personally make millions of decisions every day.

The true foundation of every complex society was therefore never violence alone.
It was information.

The history of power does not begin with the sword.
It begins with the list.

The Moment When Numbers Became More Important Than Muscles

Around ten thousand years ago, human history changed fundamentally.
Hunter-gatherers became sedentary.
Agriculture emerged.
With agriculture came a new problem.

Suddenly, people needed to know:

- Who owns which field?
- Who owes whom grain?
- How large are the supplies?
- How many animals does a family own?
- How many workers are needed?

Nature was no longer the greatest problem.
Complexity became the problem.

With every additional person, the amount of information grew exponentially.

A new need arose:
Administration.

And this is precisely where the history of invisible power begins.

Mesopotamia: The Birth of Information Rule

The first cities of Mesopotamia were not only religious centers.
They were data centers.

The temples of Uruk, Eridu, or Lagash functioned as:

- storehouses
- administrative centers
- archives
- tax authorities
- economic planning offices

In school textbooks, the temple often appears as a religious site.
In reality, it was simultaneously the first large-scale administration in human history.

The priest was not merely a mediator between humans and gods.
He was:

- bookkeeper
- logistician
- economic manager
- data steward

The temple organized society.
Religion was often the legitimizing layer above a deeper administrative apparatus.

The Invention of Writing Was Not a Literary Revolution

One of the greatest misunderstandings of history concerns writing.
Many people believe:
Writing came into being for stories.
For poems.
For philosophy.

Archaeology shows otherwise.
The oldest written characters were predominantly used for bookkeeping.
Grain.
Goats.
Working hours.
Taxes.
Deliveries.

The first scribes did not record myths.
They recorded inventory.

Writing did not arise from the desire for expression.
But from the need for control.

Before people managed ideas, they managed supplies.

The First Black Box

For the ordinary farmer, the administrative mechanisms of the temple were hardly comprehensible.
He knew:

- He delivers grain.
- The temple distributes resources.
- Decisions are made.

Yet the full logic of the system remained hidden.
Only a few people understood:

- the records
- the calculations
- the inventory planning
- the distribution keys

Here, something emerges that exists to this day:
The black box.

A system whose results are visible, but whose inner workings remain accessible only to a small elite.
Modern society thinks black boxes are a product of the computer age.
In truth, they have accompanied civilization since its very beginnings.

The Birth of the Expert Class

With complexity came a new social group.
Not the strongest.
Not the richest.
But those who mastered information.

The scribes of Mesopotamia often required years of training.
They learned:

- signs
- calculations
- administrative procedures

The majority of the population remained illiterate.
Thus, an information gap emerged.
This gap turned into power.

The scribes became the first knowledge elites in history.
They were the ancestors of:

- modern bureaucrats
- economists
- statisticians
- programmers
- data scientists

The tools changed.
The function remained the same.

Why Humans Accept Invisible Systems

Here we encounter one of the most important questions of this book.
Why do people accept systems they do not understand?

The answer is surprisingly simple.
Because these systems work.

The farmer did not need to understand how the temple calculated.
He only needed to experience that:

- supplies were available
- irrigation worked
- trade was organized

Legitimacy arose from results.
Not from transparency.

This principle has accompanied humanity to this day.
Only a few people understand:

•central banks
•global financial markets
•semiconductor production
•neural networks

Nevertheless, we accept their existence.
Because they produce results.

The modern world is based on trust in systems we cannot fully comprehend.

The Invisible Contract of Civilization

Every complex society rests on a silent exchange.
The majority forgoes complete understanding.
A minority takes over administration and organization.

In return, it promises:

•order
•stability
•prosperity

This contract was the foundation of:

- ancient empires
- medieval states
- modern democracies

But it contains a risk.
The greater the information asymmetry becomes, the greater the power of the administrators grows.
At some point, society no longer understands how the systems that support it function.
Then dependence arises.

From Temple Administration to Algorithm

At first glance, worlds seem to lie between a Mesopotamian priest and a developer of artificial intelligence.
Yet structurally, both fulfill the same role.

Both manage complexity.
Both translate reality into abstract symbols.
Both make decisions based on information that others do not fully understand.

The difference lies only in the medium.
The priest worked with clay tablets.
The developer works with databases.
The temple managed grain.
The algorithm manages capital.

The logic remains surprisingly similar.

The Real Invention

The greatest invention of Mesopotamia was therefore neither writing nor the city.
It was the realization that societies can be organized through information structures.

This discovery changed human history more profoundly than many wars or dynasties.
Because from that moment onward, power became increasingly invisible.
It migrated:
from muscle to information,
from warrior to administrator,
from visible ruler to invisible system.

The history of civilization is therefore not only the history of kings and empires.
It is the history of those hidden orders that determine who knows, who decides, and who obeys.

Chapter 2 – The Priests of Numbers

How Mathematics Became the Invisible Language of Power

"He who masters numbers, masters patterns. He who masters patterns, masters decisions. He who masters decisions, masters the world."

The Second Revolution of Power

In the previous chapter, we saw how the early high cultures gave rise to a new form of rule: rule through information.
But information alone does not yet create order.
Lists, inventory records, and tax registers can collect data, but they do not explain the world.

As early civilizations grew, a new need emerged:
Not only to know what is.
But to recognize why it happens.

Here begins the second great revolution of power.
The birth of mathematics as the universal language of reality.

The Discovery of Hidden Patterns

For the people of antiquity, the world was full of apparent coincidences.

- Seasons changed.
- Rivers overflowed their banks.
- Stars wandered across the sky.
- Harvests succeeded or failed.

But at some point, some observers recognized something astonishing:
Behind the chaos, regularities were hidden.

The sun appeared in fixed cycles.
The moon followed recurring phases.
Planets moved according to patterns.

The world was not completely chaotic.
It was ordered.
And this order could be described.
With numbers.

The Birth of the Mathematical Elite

Thus, a new form of knowledge emerged.
While the priests of Mesopotamia managed supplies, others began to investigate the very structure of reality.

The early astronomers were not scientists in the modern sense.
They were power technologists.

Whoever controlled the calendar controlled:

- sowing
- the harvest
- religious festivals
- tax deadlines

The ability to predict celestial movements conferred authority.
Not because it was magical.
But because it worked.

Prediction became the first form of scientific power.

Pythagoras and the Mysticism of Number

This becomes particularly evident with the Greek thinker Pythagoras.
Today, he is remembered for a geometric theorem.
Yet his school was far more than a mathematical academy.
It was a secret doctrine.

For Pythagoras, numbers were not tools.
They were the hidden substance of the universe.

The Pythagoreans believed:
Everything is number.
Music.
Geometry.
Astronomy.
Politics.
Even the soul.

Behind all phenomena, they suspected mathematical relationships.
This idea may seem exotic today.
In truth, it forms the foundation of modern science.
And ultimately, also of modern financial markets.

The Power of Prediction

The rulers of antiquity quickly grasped the value of mathematical knowledge.
A general who could calculate troop movements possessed advantages.
A builder who understood statics could erect monuments.
An administrator who could predict yields increased tax revenues.

Mathematics thus became a technology of the future.
It enabled for the first time:

- planning
- simulation
- forecasting

These are the same functions that modern algorithms perform today.
The tools have changed.
The logic has not.

Numbers as a New Authority

A profound shift took place.
Earlier, power was legitimized by:

- lineage
- religion
- tradition

With the spread of mathematical thinking, a new source of authority emerged:
Calculation.

No longer was the king alone right.
Rather, increasingly, the one whose model could better describe reality.

Here lies one of the roots of modern technocracies.
Legitimation shifts:
from divine truth
to mathematical precision.

The Invention of Probability

Until the Middle Ages, mathematics remained primarily the science of measurable things.
Then something revolutionary happened.
People began to calculate chance itself.

From questions of gambling, probability theory developed.
The works of thinkers such as Blaise Pascal and Pierre de Fermat led to an insight that would change the modern world:
Even uncertainty possesses structure.
Chance is not the absence of order.
It follows statistical laws.

This discovery changed everything.
Insurance.
Financial markets.
Economies.
Demographic forecasts.
Military strategies.

Modern states increasingly became machines for the administration of probability.

The Measurement of Society

In the 18th and 19th centuries, another revolution emerged.
Governments began to systematically count their populations.
Births.
Deaths.
Taxes.
Occupations.
Diseases.

For the first time, society itself became a mathematical object.
Here, statistics emerges.
The term derives from *state* (Latin: *status*).
Originally, statistics meant:
knowledge about the state.

The population became a data landscape.
People became variables.
Society became calculable.

The Birth of the Modern Oracle

Earlier cultures consulted oracles.
Modern societies consult models.
The difference appears large.
Yet structurally, the parallels are remarkable.

Both promise:

•orientation
•prediction
•decision support

When today central banks publish forecasts, when economists create growth models, or risk systems evaluate financial markets, something similar occurs as in ancient sanctuaries:
The future is translated into a language that only specialists fully understand.
The difference lies not in the function.
But in the methodology.

The Invisible Religion of Modernity

The modern world considers itself secular.
Yet it possesses its own belief systems.
One of them is the belief in numbers.

We often trust numbers more than people.
When an expert says:
"I believe ..."
we remain skeptical.
When he says:
"The data show ..."
we tend to trust him more.

Numbers create an aura of objectivity.
Yet they are always selected, interpreted, and modeled by humans.
The number appears neutral.
Its application never is.

From Mathematics to Algorithm

The development of mathematics finally led to a radical consequence.
If the world is mathematically describable,
and if machines can perform mathematical operations faster than humans,
then machines can make certain decisions better than their creators.

Here begins the direct line to the themes of this book.
For algorithms are not alien beings.
They are the latest embodiment of an ancient idea:
The hope that order can be derived from calculation.

From the Babylonian astronomer through the Pythagorean mystic to the developer of artificial intelligence, a common thread runs:
Behind the visible world exist patterns.
Whoever recognizes these patterns gains power.

The Birth of the New Priesthood

In the 21st century, we are experiencing the return of an ancient figure.
No longer in the temple.
No longer in an observatory.
No longer in a royal administration.
But in data centers, research laboratories, and financial institutions.

The new priests wear no robes.
Their tools are:

- models
- algorithms
- datasets
- neural networks

Yet their social function resembles that of their historical predecessors.
They interpret a reality that has become too complex for most people.
They translate chaos into predictions.
And they shape decisions that influence the lives of millions.

Chapter 3 – The Birth of Financial Alchemy

How numbers became money, money became power, and power became an invisible system

"The alchemist wanted to turn lead into gold. The banker discovered something far more powerful: the ability to turn promises into wealth."

The Great Transformation

The history of civilization knows many revolutions.
Agriculture turned nature into yield.
Writing turned memory into information.
Mathematics turned observation into calculation.

But at some point, an even more profound innovation emerged.
The discovery that values can exist without being materially present.

This moment marks the birth of what we today call the financial system.
And simultaneously, the birth of a new form of invisible power.

The Enigma of Money

Almost every person uses money.
Few understand what it actually is.

Most people imagine money as something concrete:

- coins
- gold
- silver
- banknotes

Yet historically, these are merely carriers.
The true essence of money lies elsewhere.

Money is trust.
Nothing more.
And nothing less.

A gold coin possesses no intrinsic value that explains its purchasing power.
A banknote is printed paper.
A digital account balance is merely a data record.

Their power arises from the shared belief in their validity.
The history of the financial system is therefore not primarily a history of wealth.
It is a history of organized belief systems.

The First Financial Priests

As early as in Mesopotamia, temples and palaces developed early credit systems.
Grain was lent.
Harvests were pre-financed.
Debts were documented.

Most people do not yet recognize modern finance in this.
Yet the basic idea was already present:
A future value was shifted into the present.

Here arose one of the most consequential discoveries of human history:
The future can be traded.

The Magic of the Promise

Let us imagine a farmer.
He needs seed.
But the harvest will not come in for months.

A loan solves this problem.
The lender accepts a promise.
No grain exists yet.
No profit exists yet.
Yet the expected result already acquires economic reality today.

This seemingly simple idea changes everything.
Because it allows for the first time:

- investments
- expansion
- trade across time periods
- economic growth

From the perspective of antiquity, this appears almost magical.
Non-existent values generate real actions.

The Alchemy of the Future

The classical alchemists sought the philosopher's stone.
They wanted to transform matter.

The financial world discovered another form of transmutation.
It turned time into capital.

Every loan is at its core a bet on the future.
Every investment is an evaluation of possibilities.
Every market price contains expectations about events that have not yet occurred.

Thus, financial markets became machines for calculating the future.
Long before computers existed.

The Medici and the Architecture of Trust

In the Europe of the Middle Ages and the Renaissance, this development took on new forms. This becomes particularly evident with the family of Cosimo de' Medici and the Medici Bank.

Their true innovation did not lie in the possession of gold.
But in the organization of trust.

A merchant could deposit money in Florence.
And access it in Bruges or London.
Not because gold was transported.
But because a network of agreements existed.

Material wealth increasingly receded into the background.
Information became more important than metal.

The Dematerialization of Power

Here begins a pattern that continues to the present day.
The more complex the financial system became, the less it depended on physical resources.

Power migrated:
from gold
to documents,

from documents
to ledgers,
from ledgers
to computers,
from computers
to algorithms.

The history of the financial system is simultaneously the history of the increasing dematerialization of power.

The Invention of the Central Bank

With the rise of modern states, a new challenge emerged.
Who controls trust itself?

The answer was:
Central banks.

Institutions such as the Bank of England created a new order.
Individual bankers no longer guaranteed stability.
Rather, institutions did.

Thus, a new form of collective belief emerged.
People no longer trusted individual persons.
But abstract systems.

This marks a crucial step toward modern financial architecture.

The Invisible Character of Money

The more successful financial systems became, the more invisible their mechanisms grew.
Most citizens today do not understand:

- money creation
- interbank trading
- government bonds
- derivatives
- central bank balances

Yet they trust these systems.
Why?
Because they work.
Or at least give the impression of working.

Here we encounter once again the basic pattern of hidden order:
Legitimacy arises not from understanding.
But from stability.

The Birth of Financial Mathematics

In the 19th and 20th centuries, the world of numbers merges with the world of money.
Mathematicians enter the financial markets.
Insurance companies calculate risks.
Banks model credit defaults.
Investors analyze probabilities.

The financial world begins to speak the language of mathematics.
This fundamentally changes its character.
Money is no longer merely managed.
It is modeled.

The Dream of Perfect Prediction

With every new mathematical method, an ancient dream grows:
To make the future calculable.

If risks can be measured,
then they can be controlled.
If markets can be modeled,
then they can be optimized.
If behavior can be predicted,
then profits can be maximized.

This dream has driven the development of the modern financial world up to the present day.
It is the real driving force behind:

- econometrics
- portfolio theory
- risk models
- artificial intelligence
- quantum optimization

The Hidden Metaphysics of the Market

Over time, the market begins to take on characteristics that go far beyond its economic function.
It becomes the highest authority of valuation.
Political decisions are measured against it.
Companies orient themselves by it.
States fear its reactions.

Governments speak of:

- market confidence
- market expectations
- market sentiment

Almost as if the market possessed its own will.
The market becomes the modern deity of the economy.
Not because people worship it.
But because they submit to its judgments.

The First Great Misconception

Yet here a dangerous fallacy arises.
People begin to believe:
If the models become complex enough,
then uncertainty will disappear.

History repeatedly disproves this hope.
Every financial crisis teaches the same lesson:
Complexity does not eliminate uncertainty.
It merely shifts it.
Often to places that no one sees anymore.

The Alchemists of Modernity

In the Middle Ages, alchemists worked in secrecy.
They searched for secret formulas.

Today, a new class of alchemists exists.
Their laboratories are:

- investment banks
- hedge funds
- research centers
- data centers

Their tools are:

- models
- algorithms
- data
- simulations

Their mission remains astonishingly similar.
They try to generate wealth from knowledge.
Predictability from uncertainty.
The present from the future.

From Financial Alchemy to the Machine Economy

The story of this chapter shows a decisive shift.
Originally, power rested on possession.
Then on information.
Then on calculation.

Now a new phase begins.
Machines increasingly take over those tasks once reserved for the financial alchemists.
The models become more complex.
The calculations faster.
The decisions more autonomous.

Step by step, humans move away from the center of the system.

Concluding Observation

The greatest innovation of financial history was not money.
Not the bank.
Not the stock exchange.
It was the discovery that the future is tradable.

This discovery created the modern world.
Yet at the same time, it produced a system whose internal mechanisms are increasingly difficult to see through.

Financial alchemy began as the art of organizing trust.
Today, it is developing into the science of algorithmic prediction.

And that is precisely where the next great transformation begins.
Because if the future can be calculated, a new question arises:
What happens when it is no longer humans but machines that calculate the future?

With this question, we enter the next section of our journey:
The machines take over.

Chapter 4 – The Death of the Floor Trader

How the Machines Entered the Market and Man Became a Spectator

"There was a time when the market was a place. Today, it is a process."

The End of an Era

When people think of stock exchanges, they often see the same images:
Men in colorful jackets.

Frantic gestures.
Shouting traders.
Paper slips.
Telephones.
An atmosphere of controlled chaos.

These images shaped the idea of how markets work for over a century.
But this world hardly exists anymore.
It was not destroyed by a crisis.
Not by a revolution.
Not by a law.
It disappeared silently.
Line by line.
Terminal by terminal.
Algorithm by algorithm.

The death of the floor trader was not an event.
It was a process.
And with it began one of the greatest power shifts in economic history.

The Stock Exchange as Theater of Modernity

The classical stock exchanges were far more than trading places.
They were public performances of economic power.

Whoever entered the trading floor entered a symbolic space.
Here, the following met:

- banks
- companies
- traders
- speculators

The market had faces.
One could observe:

- fear
- greed
- panic
- euphoria

Human psychology was visible.
The stock exchange was a stage upon which the emotions of capitalism were publicly performed.

The Illusion of Human Control

This world produced a powerful notion:
That markets are made by humans.

The trader was seen as the central figure.
He observed.
Evaluated.

Decided.
Acted.

The public imagined the market as the sum of individual decisions.
Yet even in this phase, reality was more complex.
Because behind every trader stood:

- banks
- rules
- networks
- information systems

The visible actors were only the surface of a deeper structure.

The Computer Enters the Stage

In the 1970s and 1980s, a silent revolution begins.
Computers become powerful enough to process financial data electronically.

At first, they appear harmless.
They help with:

- accounting
- data analysis
- price calculation

No one speaks of a takeover.
The computer seems like a tool.

An assistant.
An aid.

But every technical support contains a hidden dynamic:
What first supports, later begins to replace.

The Birth of Electronic Markets

With the emergence of electronic trading platforms, the nature of the market changes fundamentally.
Suddenly, physical presence is no longer necessary.
The trader no longer has to stand on the floor.
A terminal suffices.
Then a network.
Then a software.
Then an algorithm.

With each step, the human is moved further away from the actual trading process.
The market loses its place.
It becomes digital.

Speed as the New Currency

For a long time, competition was based on knowledge.
Whoever had better information won.

With digitalization, a new resource emerges:
Speed.
Not seconds.
Not milliseconds.
But microseconds.
Later, nanoseconds.

Suddenly, a race begins that changes the logic of markets.
The question is no longer:
Who knows more?
But rather:
Who reacts faster?

Time becomes a commodity.

The Emergence of High-Frequency Trading

From this race, high-frequency trading emerges.
High Frequency Trading.
HFT.
A new species of the market.

These systems analyze:

- prices

- volumes
- news
- order books

and react within timeframes that have become irrelevant to humans.
A human blink lasts about 300 milliseconds.
In the same time, modern trading systems can make millions of decisions.

For the first time, a fundamental asymmetry arises.
The human not only loses speed.
He loses his relevance.

The Moment of Disempowerment

There is no single day when the machines took control.
But at some point, it became clear:
The human can no longer compete.
Not because he is dumber.
But because he is biologically limited.

The human nervous system has a fixed speed.
The machine knows no such limit.

The competition does not end with this.
It becomes meaningless.
It is like pitting a runner against light.

The Market Ceases to Be Human

At this point, something deeper than mere automation occurs.
The logic of the market changes.

Humans act based on:

- expectations
- beliefs
- narratives
- emotions

Machines act based on:

- patterns
- probabilities
- optimization functions
- mathematical states

The market begins to respond to signals that were never intended for human perception.
It becomes increasingly controlled by a language that humans can neither see nor intuitively understand.

The Flash Crash as Revelation

On May 6, 2010, something occurs that seems like a glimpse behind the curtain.

Within minutes, US markets temporarily lose nearly one trillion dollars in value.
Then they recover.

Many people experience this moment as a shock.
Not because of the losses.
But because of a realization:
No one fully understood what had just happened.

Machines reacted to machines.
Algorithms amplified algorithms.
The market began to communicate with itself.
Humans became observers of a process they no longer controlled.

The Flash Crash was not simply a technical problem.
It was a philosophical event.

The Birth of Black-Box Markets

The more complex the systems become, the more difficult their traceability.
In the past, a trader could explain:
Why he bought.
Why he sold.
Why he took a risk.

A neural network often cannot do this.
A self-learning model makes decisions based on

high-dimensional relationships.
The decision is visible.
The reasoning disappears.

Here emerges the financial world we called "algorithmic esotericism" in the prologue.

The New Elite

With the disappearance of the floor trader, power does not disappear.
It shifts.

The winners of the new order are no longer the loudest actors.
But rather those who:

- develop models
- possess data
- control data centers
- optimize networks

The classical trader is replaced by:

- quantitative analysts
- mathematicians
- physicists
- computer scientists

The stock exchange turns from a marketplace into a laboratory.

The Invisible Market

Today, the market exists largely outside human perception.
Not on screens.
Not in news.
But in data centers.
Between servers.
In fiber-optic cables.
In data packets.

The modern market is no longer a place.
It is an infrastructure.
A permanent, global computing operation.

The True Meaning of the Death

The death of the floor trader does not merely signify the end of a profession.
It marks the end of a worldview.

For centuries, we believed:
Markets are places of human decisions.

Today, we must recognize:
Markets are evolving into systems of machine interactions.

Humans remain owners.
Sometimes regulators.
Often spectators.
But increasingly rarely direct actors.

Concluding Observation

The history of financial markets is not only a history of money.
It is the history of the shifting of decision-making power.
From merchant to banker.
From banker to mathematician.
From mathematician to algorithm.

The death of the floor trader was therefore more than a technological change.
It was the moment when the financial world began to detach itself from the limits of human perception.

And that is precisely where the next phase of our investigation begins:
No longer the question of whether machines can act.
But rather:

What happens when speed itself becomes the dominant form of power?

With that, we enter the age of high-frequency trading – the conquest of time.

Chapter 5 – High Frequency and the Conquest of Time

How Microseconds Became the Most Valuable Resource in the Financial World

"In the past, traders competed for knowledge. Today, machines compete for time."

The Final Frontier

Every era possesses its decisive resource.
For agrarian societies, it was land.
For industrial societies, it was energy.
For the information age, it was data.

But in high-frequency trading, a new resource appears, one that is even more fundamental: Time.

Not time in the human sense.
Not hours.
Not days.
Not even seconds.

But time as a physical quantity.
Time as a measurable distance between signal and decision.
Time as a raw material.

The Invisibility of Speed

For humans, speed exists only up to a certain point.
We notice the difference between a minute and an hour.
Between a second and a minute.
But somewhere, our perception ends.

No one can intuitively grasp what a microsecond means.
A microsecond is one millionth of a second.
A nanosecond is one billionth.

In these realms, human experience loses its footing.
We enter a world that is completely machinic.
There, no emotions exist.
No reflection.

No intuition.
Only signals.

The Discovery of the Time Advantage

The first algorithmic traders noticed something surprising.
The difference between profits and losses often lay not in better analyses.
But in faster execution.

If two market participants possess the same information, the one who acts first often wins.
This seems trivial.
Yet the consequences were revolutionary.

Suddenly, every millisecond became an asset.
Speed became tradable.

Physics Takes Over Economics

Until this point, finance was primarily a discipline of mathematics.
Now, a new science enters the scene:
Physics.

High-frequency trading forces financial actors to engage with questions once reserved for engineers:

- How fast does light travel?
- How long is a fiber-optic cable?
- Which route does the signal take?
- How much delay does the hardware cause?

The market begins to move closer to the laws of relativity than to those of classical economics.
It is not the smartest trader who wins.
But often the one whose signal arrives first.

The Geography of Speed

With high-frequency trading, the meaning of space changes.
In the past, distance between market participants hardly mattered.
Today, it can cost millions.

That is why new forms of infrastructural power emerge:

- Servers are placed directly next to exchanges.
- Fiber-optic cables are straightened.
- Microwave links cut through landscapes.
- Data centers arise at strategic hubs.

This practice becomes known as co-location.
Proximity to the market itself becomes a market good.
Whoever is closer sees first.
Whoever sees first, acts first.

The War for Nanoseconds

In earlier centuries, wars were fought over territories.
In high-frequency trading, a war for nanoseconds begins.

Companies invest billions to gain minimal time advantages.
Some examples seem almost absurd:

- Drilling through mountains to shorten cables.
- Special radio connections over long distances.
- Proprietary satellite communication.
- Custom-designed processors.

From a human perspective, this appears irrational.
Why invest billions to gain microseconds?
The answer is:
Because in a market of billions of transactions, even minimal advantages have exponential effects.

The New Form of Knowledge

Traditionally, knowledge was a content.
Something one understood.

In high-frequency trading, a new form of knowledge emerges.
Not:
What do you know?
but rather:
When do you know it?

The time advantage becomes more important than the content of the information.
A signal that arrives a few microseconds earlier possesses economic value.
Time becomes information.
Information becomes capital.

The Market as a Nervous System

With increasing speed, the market begins to take on characteristics of a biological system.
It increasingly resembles less a trading place.
And more a nervous system.

Signals arise.
They are transmitted.
They trigger reactions.
New signals arise.
New reactions follow.

This cycle happens continuously.
Billions of times.

The market develops reflexes.
Not in the human sense.
But as an emergent property of networked algorithms.

The Birth of the Machine Ecology

A crucial shift often goes unnoticed.
Algorithms no longer primarily act against humans.
They act against each other.

The majority of signals are generated by machines.
The majority of reactions are carried out by machines.
The majority of market communication takes place between machines.

The human increasingly steps out of the cycle.
A new ecological order emerges:
A machine ecology.

Within this order, systems compete for:

- speed
- efficiency
- predictive power

The human becomes a distant observer.

The Illusion of Perfect Efficiency

Proponents of high-frequency trading often argue:
More speed means better markets.

Indeed, HFT brings real advantages:

- lower spreads
- higher liquidity
- faster price formation

Yet these advantages have a dark side.
The more markets are optimized, the more sensitively they can react to disturbances.

A highly optimized system often has less fault tolerance.
Just as a race car is more powerful but more fragile than a truck.

The Flash Crash as Time Collapse

The Flash Crash of 2010 reveals this problem.
Within minutes, prices collapse.
Then they stabilize again.

But more important than the losses is the cause.
Speed itself becomes the risk.

Algorithms react to algorithms.
Feedback loops amplify signals.
The dynamics develop faster than humans can intervene.

The timeframes of human decision-making become irrelevant.
A time collapse occurs.
The market moves on a level beyond human control.

The Emergence of a New Ontology

Traditional economics views markets as places of exchange.
High-frequency trading changes this view.

The market becomes an information field.
Prices are no longer merely valuations.
They become signals.
Liquidity becomes information.
Volatility becomes communication.

The market transforms into a giant distributed computing system.
A global machine for processing expectations.

The Philosophical Significance of Speed

Here we reach a deeper point.
High-frequency trading not only changes the markets.
It changes the relationship between humans and reality.

For thousands of years, human perception was the foundation of all decisions.
Now, processes are emerging that operate completely outside this perception.

This means:
Power is beginning to detach itself from experience.

In the past, a trader could observe, understand, and act.
Today, the action often occurs before understanding.
The machine reacts.
The human only interprets afterwards.
The order is reversed.

The Conquest of Time

Historically, empires conquered:

- territories

- trade routes
- resources

High-frequency trading conquers something more fundamental:
Time itself.
Not by stopping it.
But by making its smallest units economically exploitable.

The microsecond becomes the new frontier of economic expansion.
Where past societies colonized land, the algorithmic financial world colonizes time.

The Prelude to Algorithmic Esotericism

Yet speed alone is not the end of the development.
It is merely the preparation.

The race for time inevitably leads to a new question:
When speed eventually reaches physical limits, where does the next advantage lie?

The answer is:
Not calculating faster.
But thinking differently.

Here begins the transition from speed to complexity.
From high-frequency trading to artificial intelligence.
From reactive systems to learning systems.
From the optimization of time to the optimization of reality itself.

PART II – THE ALGORITHMIC PRIESTS

Chapter 6 – The Black Box Society

How the Logic of Algorithms Became the Invisible Infrastructure of Modernity

"The greatest power is not that which hides. The greatest power is that which is visible but no one understands anymore."

The End of Explainability

The history of modernity was for a long time the history of increasing transparency.
The Enlightenment promised:

- knowledge instead of myth
- science instead of superstition
- reason instead of authority

The basic assumption was:
If we understand the world better, we will master it better.

For centuries, this hope seemed to be fulfilled.
Machines became more complex.

Institutions grew larger.
Societies became more interconnected.

Yet at the same time, an unexpected paradox emerged:
The more successful our systems became, the harder they became to understand.

Today, we live in a world whose most important decisions are increasingly made by processes that elude human comprehension.
We are entering the age of the black box.

What Is a Black Box?

The term originally comes from engineering.
A black box is a system whose inputs and outputs are known, but whose inner workings remain hidden.

One sees:

- What goes in.
- What comes out.

But the path in between remains unclear.

In early technology, this was often merely a practical simplification.
With modern algorithms, it becomes a structural

problem.
Because the black box is not hidden because someone is hiding it.
It is hidden because its complexity exceeds human reconstruction.

The Old and the New Opacity

Historically, two forms of not-knowing existed.
The first was secrecy.
Rulers withheld information.
Priests guarded secret knowledge.
Bankers protected their books.
This was a political form of opacity.

The second form is new.
No one has to hide anything.
The source code may be open.
The data may be public.
And yet the system remains incomprehensible.

Why?
Because complexity itself has become a barrier.

We are experiencing the transition from secrecy to hypercomplexity.

The Return of the Oracle

In antiquity, people consulted oracles.
They received answers whose origin they could not comprehend.

Today, we consult search engines, recommendation systems, and AI models.
The difference seems enormous.
Yet structurally, astonishing parallels exist.

We ask a question.
We receive an answer.
We trust the result.
The inner logic remains hidden.

Of course, modern systems are based on mathematics, not mythology.
But for the user, this often makes no difference.
The experience remains the same:
An authority provides orientation without its thought process becoming visible.

The Birth of Algorithmic Authority

One of the deepest changes of the present is that decisions are increasingly delegated to models.
In the past, humans made decisions using information.

Today, systems make decisions using human information.

This difference seems small.
In truth, it changes the structure of power.

Examples can be found everywhere:

- creditworthiness assessments
- insurance premiums
- applicant screening
- facial recognition
- medical diagnostics
- financial trading

The algorithm becomes a silent co-decision-maker.
Not as an advisor.
But increasingly as an authority.

The Invisibility of Influence

Most people do not experience algorithms as rule.
They experience them as convenience.

A recommendation on a platform.
A navigation route.
A search query.
A product suggestion.
A personalized news feed.

But it is precisely this invisibility that makes their influence so effective.
Power is most effective when it is not perceived as power.

The user believes they are choosing freely.
While the range of choices has already been structured.
The decision remains individual.
The decision environment does not.

From Statistics to Prediction

Classical statistics described the past.
Modern systems attempt to predict the future.
This is a fundamental difference.

A neural network is not primarily interested in truth.
It is interested in hit probability.
It does not ask:
Why is something happening?
But rather:
What is likely to happen?

Thus, the logic of knowledge shifts.
Explanation becomes less important.
Prediction becomes more important.
Society begins to value predictive power more highly than understanding.

The Crisis of Causality

Here arises one of the central problems of the 21st century.
Humans think in causes.
Algorithms think in correlations.

A human asks:
What causes this event?
A model asks:
Which patterns frequently precede this event?

The difference is enormous.
Correlation requires no understanding.
It merely requires sufficient data.

Thus, systems emerge that can successfully predict without knowing why something happens.
We are moving from a causal to a probabilistic culture.

Society as Data Shadow

To make predictions, systems must collect data.
Much more data than past societies could ever generate.

Every click.
Every purchase.
Every movement.

Every search query.
Every interaction.

From these traces, a second image of the human emerges.
A digital twin.
A data shadow.

This data shadow becomes increasingly more important than the physical person themselves.
Because the systems do not make decisions about humans.
They make decisions about their data representations.

The New Form of Power

Traditionally, power was based on control over people.
Today, it is increasingly based on control over models.

Whoever owns the models:

- interprets behavior,
- assesses risks,
- defines relevance,
- steers attention.

The new power rarely acts directly.
It shapes probabilities.
It changes incentives.
It forms decision spaces.

This makes it difficult to see.
And difficult to attack.

The Financial Markets as Pioneers

As so often, these developments appear first in the financial world.
Modern trading has long been based on models that no single person fully comprehends.

Algorithms analyze:

- price movements
- liquidity flows
- news
- social signals
- macroeconomic data

and generate decisions in real time.

The financial markets are thus the first fully algorithmized environment of modernity.
They show what many other areas of society could later achieve.

The Paradox of Rationality

Modernity believed:
More data leads to more rationality.
More calculation leads to more control.
More knowledge leads to more understanding.

Reality is developing differently.
More data often generates more complexity.
More models generate more opacity.
More calculation generates more dependency.

The result is paradoxical:
The most rational society in history produces new forms of not-knowing.

Algorithmic Esotericism

At this point, we return to the central thesis of this book.
Esotericism originally meant:
Knowledge for an inner circle.

Today, a new form of this principle is emerging.
Not because knowledge is kept secret.
But because only a few people possess the skills to understand the systems at all.

The new initiates are:

- mathematicians
- data scientists
- AI researchers
- quants
- system architects

They do not form a conspiracy.
Yet they form a knowledge elite.
And every knowledge elite creates power asymmetries.

The Illusion of Neutrality

One of the most dangerous assumptions of our time is:
Algorithms are neutral.

In truth, models always contain decisions.
Which data is collected?
Which goals are optimized?
Which risks are accepted?
Which errors are tolerated?

Each of these decisions is human.
The algorithm appears objective.
Its architecture is not.

Society in the Mirror of the Machine

Perhaps the deepest significance of the black box lies not in the machines themselves.
But in what they reveal about us.

Algorithms are not alien beings.
They are condensations of human decisions.
Condensations of human values.
Condensations of human priorities.

The black box not only reflects our technology.
It reflects our society.

The more precisely we look into it, the more clearly we recognize:
The real opacity lies not in the code.
It lies in the power structures, interests, and assumptions that we have inscribed into the code.

Concluding Observation

The black box society marks a historical turning point.
For the first time, humanity is creating systems that are not powerful because they exert violence.
But because they organize complexity.

The question is therefore no longer:
Who holds power?

But rather:
Who holds the models that determine how power is exercised?

With this question, the story of machines as tools ends.
And the story of algorithms as structures of rule begins.

Chapter 7 – The New High Council

Whoever Controls the Infrastructure, Controls Reality

"The most powerful people of an era are often not those who rule visibly, but those who determine how decisions are made in the first place."

The False Idea of Power

When people speak of power, they usually think of the visible actors.
Of:

- presidents
- ministers
- monarchs

- billionaires
- generals

History shows, however, a recurring pattern:
The most visible actors are rarely the only centers of power.

Behind every political order exists a deeper level.
A level of:

- institutions
- networks
- information structures
- resource flows

This level often determines which decisions are even possible.

In the age of algorithms, power is shifting once again.
Not away from states.
Not away from corporations.
But deeper into the infrastructure of reality itself.

The Architecture Behind the Architecture

Most people experience technology as a surface.
They see:

- apps

- websites
- search engines
- social networks
- digital payment systems

But every surface rests on a deeper structure.
Below every application exist:

- data centers
- cloud networks
- databases
- communication lines
- AI models
- financial systems

This infrastructure forms the nervous system of modern civilization.
Whoever controls this nervous system influences far more than individual companies.
They influence the conditions under which society functions.

The New Concentration of Power

One of the most striking developments of the 21st century is the concentration of computing power.
Historically, power was tied to physical resources:

- land
- raw materials

•factories
•trade routes

Today, new resources are emerging:

•data
•chips
•networks
•models
•computing capacity

These resources are not distributed evenly.
They gather at a few nodal points.
There, a new form of structural power emerges.
Not through territories.
But through information control.

The Invisible Rulers of Infrastructure

The modern world is carried by a layer of actors often less known to the public than politicians or celebrities.
These include:

•operators of global cloud infrastructures
•manufacturers of high-performance chips
•operators of undersea cables
•providers of AI models
•operators of large financial networks

These actors determine:

- which data can be processed,
- which models can be trained,
- which computing power is available,
- which markets are connected to each other.

They do not necessarily control content.
They control the prerequisites of its existence.

The Return of the Priest Caste

In the first chapter, we encountered the priests of Mesopotamia.
They controlled:

- writing
- accounting
- supplies
- administration

The population did not fully understand the mechanisms.
Yet they depended on them.

In the 21st century, this pattern returns in a new form.
The new priests wear no robes.
Their tools are:

- mathematical models
- programming languages
- neural networks
- quantum algorithms

Like their historical predecessors, they manage systems whose complexity overwhelms most people.

The Emergence of a Technocratic Elite

Every society produces specialists.
But not every specialist group becomes a power elite.

An elite emerges where three conditions come together:

1. Exclusive knowledge
2. Control over critical resources
3. Limited verifiability

The algorithmic elite fulfills all three conditions.
Their knowledge is highly specialized.
Their resources are central to the economy and politics.
And their decisions are often only verifiable to a limited extent.

This does not mean that they secretly rule the world.
It means that they possess a disproportionate influence on the structure of decision-making.

The Power of Models

In earlier centuries, rulers possessed armies.
Today, institutions possess models.

The difference is greater than it initially appears.
A model defines:

- which risks become visible,
- which opportunities appear relevant,
- which actions are recommended.

Models generate perception.
And perception generates decisions.

Whoever controls the models influences the reality that others see.

The Financial World as a Laboratory of Power

Nowhere is this more evident than in the financial system.
Modern capital flows are no longer directed

exclusively by humans.
They are filtered through:

- risk models
- credit ratings
- trading algorithms
- portfolio optimizations

When a country gains or loses investments, this often happens not solely because of political decisions.
Between the event and the capital flow stand models.
The models interpret the world.
The markets react to the interpretation.

The New Form of Feudalism

Some thinkers now speak of techno-feudalism.
The term is controversial, but it points to an interesting observation.

In feudalism, a small elite controlled the infrastructure of life:

- land
- water
- protection
- trade

Today, new actors control:

•data
•networks
•data centers
•digital identities

The comparison is not perfect.
Yet it makes visible that power is increasingly becoming infrastructural.
People may own their devices.
But the systems on which these devices depend mostly belong to others.

The Oligarchy of Computing Power

This becomes particularly evident in the field of artificial intelligence.
Advanced models require:

•enormous amounts of data,
•specialized hardware,
•vast amounts of energy,
•billion-dollar investments.

This creates a natural concentration.
Only a few organizations possess the necessary resources.

This leads to a paradoxical situation.
The more democratic digital technologies appear, the more concentrated the infrastructure behind them often becomes.

The Geopolitical Dimension

The New High Council is not a single body.
It is a network.

Its members sit:

- in corporate headquarters,
- research institutes,
- central banks,
- technology labs,
- government agencies.

The boundaries between economy, technology, and the state are becoming increasingly porous.
Data policy becomes geopolitics.
Chip production becomes security policy.
AI development becomes power politics.

Infrastructure becomes the strategic battlefield of the 21st century.

The Invisibility of Modern Rule

Perhaps the greatest strength of this new order lies in its invisibility.
Historical rule was visible.
Taxes were collected.
Laws were proclaimed.
Soldiers stood on the streets.

Algorithmic power works differently.
It shapes:

- recommendations
- rankings
- risk assessments
- information flows
- capital allocations

This often happens without those affected noticing the intervention.
Power does not lie in command.
It lies in the shaping of possibilities.

The Question of Legitimacy

Here we encounter a fundamental problem.
Democratic societies legitimize power through:

- elections
- laws

- public control

But how is algorithmic power legitimized?
Who elects the models?
Who controls the training data?
Who decides on optimization goals?
Who reviews the impacts?

These questions become the central political questions of the 21st century.

The High Council as a System, Not a Conspiracy

It would be a mistake to view the New High Council as a secret group.
Reality is more complex.

There is no hidden committee that steers the world.
Rather, power arises from the interweaving of:

- capital
- technology
- knowledge
- infrastructure

The New High Council is not an organization.
It is a structure.

A network of institutions and actors that together shape the conditions of modern reality.

The Real Transformation

The deepest change is not that a few are becoming more powerful.
But that power itself is changing its character.

In the past, power meant:
Controlling people.

Today, power increasingly means:
Controlling systems that influence people.

Control shifts from individuals to architectures.
From commands to probabilities.
From direct rule to infrastructural design.

Concluding Observation

The New High Council does not rule like kings.
It issues no decrees.
It demands no obedience.

Its power operates more subtly.
It controls the systems through which information flows, decisions arise, and capital moves.

Thus, it becomes the central actor of a new historical epoch.
An epoch in which power becomes less visible, but no less effective.

Chapter 8 – The New Secret Language

How Code Became the Language of Power

"Every epoch possesses a language that only a few understand. Whoever masters this language can not only describe the world – they can change it."

The Oldest Pattern of Power

The history of civilization is also the history of privileged languages.
In early tribal societies, knowledge was largely communal.
With the emergence of complex societies, this changed.

Certain groups developed exclusive writing systems, specialized languages, and forms of knowledge.
Not everyone could read.
Not everyone could write.

Not everyone was allowed to interpret the sacred texts.

Language became an instrument of power.
Because language does more than transmit information.
It determines what can be thought at all.

Writing as the First Secret Language

When the first scribes of Mesopotamia developed cuneiform, a new social division emerged.
On one side stood those who could read signs.
On the other side stood those who had to trust them.

The majority of the population had no direct access to:

- tax lists
- contracts
- property records
- administrative documents

Writing was not a neutral tool.
It was an infrastructure of power.
The scribe became the mediator between reality and documentation.

Latin and the Administration of Knowledge

Centuries later, Latin took on a similar role.
In medieval Europe, Latin was the language of:

- the Church
- science
- administration
- law

Most people could not understand it.
Yet decisions about their lives were formulated in this language.

A priest read the Holy Scripture.
A jurist drafted contracts.
A scholar wrote scientific treatises.

Between knowledge and the population existed a linguistic barrier.
This barrier created authority.

Mathematics as the Universal Priestly Language

With the scientific revolution, a new language emerged.
The language of numbers.

Mathematics possessed a decisive advantage.
It was more precise than natural language.
It allowed:

- calculations
- predictions
- models
- technical constructions

Yet at the same time, a new problem arose.
The more powerful mathematics became, the fewer people could follow it.

Modern society accepted this because the results worked.
Airplanes flew.
Bridges held.
Electricity functioned.

The authority of mathematics rested on its effectiveness.

The Rise of Code

In the 20th century, another language appears.
At first, it seems technical.
Inconspicuous.
Limited to scientists and engineers.

This language is called:
Code.

Initially, it served merely to give commands to machines.
But gradually, something unexpected happens.
Code leaves the machine.
And begins to organize society.

When Language Creates Reality

Natural language describes the world.
Code changes it directly.

This difference is crucial.
When a law is passed, it must be interpreted.
When a program is executed, it directly generates an action.

Code possesses an operational force.
It does not merely describe rules.
It implements them.

Thus, for the first time, a language emerges that is simultaneously prescription and execution.

"Code is Law"

Computer scientist and legal scholar Lawrence Lessig coined a famous phrase:
Code is Law.

He meant:
Digital systems regulate behavior similarly to laws.

A law can prohibit opening a door.
Code can simply keep the door locked.

A law can forbid access.
Code can make access technically impossible.

Here begins a new form of power.
Not the power of prescription.
But the power of architecture.

The Invisible Legislators

In a digital society, rules increasingly emerge through technical design.
Programmers decide:

- which functions are available,
- which information becomes visible,
- which interactions are allowed,
- which actions are blocked.

These decisions often seem purely technical.
In fact, they have political consequences.

Every architecture contains values.
Every algorithm contains priorities.
Every platform contains assumptions about how people should act.

The Priests of the Digital Temple

Like earlier priests, developers possess a special ability.
They can translate abstract symbols into real effects.

A few lines of code can:

- move billions,
- control communication,
- influence markets,
- control infrastructure.

Of course, the majority of developers do not work with such intentions.
Yet the societal impact remains.

Whoever writes code increasingly shapes the conditions of reality.

The New Illiteracy Question

In the Middle Ages, illiteracy meant not being able to read.
In the digital age, a new form emerges.

Many people can read texts.
Yet they cannot read the systems that structure their daily lives.

They understand:

- the surface,
- but not the logic beneath it.

They use:

- apps,
- platforms,
- financial systems,
- AI tools,

without being able to comprehend how they work.

This creates a new dependency.
Not on the literate.
But on the system-literate.

The Language of Machines

Another shift is occurring.
In the past, humans wrote code for machines.
Today, machines increasingly write code for humans.

Artificial intelligence generates:

- programs,
- models,
- optimizations,
- decision rules.

Thus, a new phase begins.
The secret language itself becomes partly automated.
The priests lose their monopoly over the liturgy.
The liturgy begins to write itself.

The Financial Markets as Code Space

Nowhere is the power of code more evident than in the modern financial system.

Today's market consists of:

- trading algorithms,
- risk models,
- smart contracts,

- data feeds,
- automated strategies.

Capital no longer moves primarily based on human conversations.
It moves based on code.

Contracts are executed by machines.
Decisions are made by machines.
Liquidity is generated by machines.

The financial world is increasingly becoming a vast program.

The Emergence of Digital Rituals

Historical religions knew rituals.
Certain actions had to be performed in a specific sequence.

The digital world knows similar structures.
Logins.
Authentications.
Payment processes.
Smart contracts.
Automated workflows.

The user performs actions.
The system reacts according to fixed rules.

The difference lies not in the existence of rituals.
But in the fact that rituals are now monitored by machines.

The Limits of Transparency

Many believe open source could solve the problem.
Open code is undoubtedly important.
But transparency alone is not enough.

A modern AI system can contain millions or billions of parameters.
Even if every part of the program were public, only a few people could understand the entirety.

The challenge of the 21st century is therefore not only secrecy.
It is cognitive overload.

Systems become complex faster than human understanding can grow.

The Emergence of a New Clerical Class

Historically, clergy emerged where knowledge was scarce.
Today, a new knowledge elite is emerging.

Not because of secret texts.
But because of technical complexity.

Their tools are:

- mathematics
- computer science
- data science
- artificial intelligence

They do not form a closed class.
Yet they possess skills that have become indispensable for modern societies.
This creates structural power.

The Metaphysics of Code

On a deeper level, code fulfills a function once held by religion and philosophy.
It answers questions such as:

- What is permitted?
- What is possible?
- What is visible?
- What is relevant?

Code defines the boundaries of digital reality.
It becomes the grammar of a new world.

Most people do not speak this language.
And yet they live in the realities it generates.

Concluding Observation

Every epoch possesses its secret language.
For the priests of Mesopotamia, it was writing.
For the scholars of the Middle Ages, Latin.
For the scientists of modernity, mathematics.
For digital civilization, it is code.

But code is more than a language.
It is architecture.
It is a rule system.
It is an instrument of power.

And above all:
It is the interface between idea and reality.

Those who master it do not only write programs.
They write the conditions under which society functions.

Chapter 9 – Algorithmic Theology

How Models Take on the Role of Oracles, Priests, and Gods

"The most powerful belief systems are not those that believe in the supernatural. The most powerful belief systems are those that no longer recognize themselves as belief systems."

The Return of the Old Questions

Every civilization eventually faces the same questions:

- Where does order come from?
- Who knows the future?
- Who interprets the invisible?
- Who decides what is true?

The answers have changed over the course of history.
In earlier times, they were:

- the gods,
- the priests,
- the prophets,
- the oracles.

Later, these answers were replaced by:

- science,
- statistics,
- economics,
- technology.

Yet the fundamental questions never disappeared.
They merely changed their language.

The Myth of the Disenchanted World

Modernity likes to tell itself a story.
It is the story of disenchantment.
The notion that science and reason have displaced the old myths.
That we now view the world objectively.
Without faith.
Without rituals.
Without priesthoods.

But this story is only partially true.
Because every society needs systems to reduce uncertainty.
Humans cannot live permanently in radical uncertainty.
They seek orientation.
They seek predictability.
They seek meaning.

The question, therefore, is not whether a society possesses belief systems.
But which ones.

The Birth of Statistical Providence

With the emergence of modern statistics, something revolutionary happens.
For the first time, the future becomes mathematically addressable.

Of course, no one can know the future exactly.
Yet probabilities create something new:
a calculable form of uncertainty.

Insurance emerges.
Stock markets emerge.
Risk management emerges.

Modern humans begin to trust statistics as earlier cultures trusted stargazers.
Not because it is infallible.
But because it works better than pure chance.

The New Oracle

In antiquity, people pilgrimaged to Delphi.
They sought answers to questions about the future.

Today, other sanctuaries exist.
Research centers.
Data centers.
Financial centers.
AI labs.

There, models are created that are supposed to answer:

- Which stock will rise?
- Which disease will occur?
- Which region will grow?
- Which person will be creditworthy?
- Which information will be relevant?

The mechanism has changed.
The function, remarkably little.

From Truth to Probability

Classical religions asked:
What is true?

The algorithmic world asks:
What is likely?

This difference marks one of the greatest cultural transformations in human history.
Modern society increasingly organizes itself not around certainties.
But around probabilities.

Elections.
Insurance.
Financial markets.
Artificial intelligence.
All operate on this basis.

The center of reality shifts.
From truth to prediction.

The Priests of Probability

In every religion, specialists exist.
People who interpret signs.
Decipher texts.
Explain connections.

In the algorithmic order, this role is taken on by:

- data scientists
- quant analysts
- AI researchers

- statisticians
- model architects

They do not read holy scriptures.
They read datasets.
They do not interpret omens.
They interpret patterns.

Yet their social function bears astonishing similarities.
They translate uncertainty into recommendations for action.

The Liturgy of Data

Religions have rituals.
They structure the relationship between humans and the invisible.

The algorithmic world also knows rituals.
Data collection.
Data cleaning.
Model training.
Validation.
Optimization.
Deployment.
Monitoring.

To outsiders, these processes often appear just as inscrutable as the religious ceremonies of past

centuries.
The rituals have changed.
The social function remains remarkably constant.

The Invisible Gods

Historical gods were invisible.
Their existence was inferred from their effects.
The rain fell.
The harvest succeeded.
A war was won.

Today, new invisible actors are emerging.
Algorithms.
Models.
Neural networks.

They possess no personality.
No intention.
No will.

And yet they influence:

- credit approvals,
- market movements,
- information flows,
- political communication,
- economic decisions.

Their existence, too, is experienced through their effects.

The Crisis of Interpretability

A central property of modern AI systems is that their decisions are often not fully explainable.
This creates a remarkable phenomenon.

People trust results they cannot comprehend.
Similar to how earlier societies trusted religious authorities.

Of course, the basis is different.
Yet structurally, the same tension arises:
We accept decisions whose inner logic eludes our understanding.

The Dogmas of the Digital Age

Every theology has basic assumptions.
The algorithmic order does as well.

Among its unspoken dogmas are often:

- More data is better.
- More computation is better.
- More optimization is better.

- Prediction is more valuable than explanation.
- Efficiency is a universal measure.

These assumptions seem self-evident to many.
Yet they are not natural laws.
They are cultural decisions.
And every cultural decision deserves critical examination.

The Original Sin of Models

Every religion knows the concept of human imperfection.
Models, too, possess a form of original sin.

They arise from data of the past.
Therefore, they reproduce:

- historical distortions,
- existing power structures,
- social inequalities,
- systemic errors.

The model appears objective.
Yet it bears the traces of its genesis.
It does not look at the world as it could be.
But at the world as it was.

The Financial Markets as Temples of Prediction

Nowhere is algorithmic theology more evident than in the financial world.
Modern markets rest on a collective act of faith: The conviction that future developments are modelable.

Every trade contains an implicit statement about the future.
Every risk model formulates a theory about uncertainty.
Every algorithm contains an idea of how the world works.

Financial markets are therefore not merely economic systems.
They are giant machines for producing future expectations.

The New Providence

Historical religions spoke of divine providence.
Of an order that worked behind events.

The algorithmic society is developing a secular variant of this idea.
The belief that sufficient data and sufficient computing power can make visible the hidden structures of reality.

This belief drives:

- artificial intelligence,
- predictive analytics,
- quantum optimization,
- algorithmic trading.

It forms the spiritual core of the new epoch.

The Difference Between God and Model

At this point, an important distinction is necessary. Models are not gods.

They possess:

- no consciousness,
- no morality,
- no intention.

The real danger, therefore, does not lie in the models themselves.
But in ascribing to them properties they do not possess.

When societies begin to believe that models are objective, neutral, and infallible, a new form of dogmatism emerges.
Not religious dogmatism.
But technical dogmatism.

The Emergence of a New Metaphysics

Every era develops ideas about how the world works at its core.
For antiquity, it was gods.
For the Middle Ages, divine order.
For the Enlightenment, natural laws.

For the information age, new concepts are emerging:

- networks,
- data streams,
- probabilities,
- information fields,
- algorithms.

These concepts become the metaphysical building blocks of the present.
They not only explain the world.
They define what counts as explainable.

The Real Question

The most important question, therefore, is not:
Are algorithms becoming more powerful?
That is already happening.

The real question is:
Which values do we inscribe into these systems?

Because every technology amplifies the goals set for it.
If efficiency is the highest goal, it amplifies efficiency.
If control is the highest goal, it amplifies control.
If fairness is the highest goal, it amplifies fairness.

The future will not be decided by technology alone.
But by the values that shape its architecture.

Concluding Observation

Algorithmic theology is not a religion in the traditional sense.
It has no temples.
No holy scriptures.
No priesthood in the classical understanding.

Yet it fulfills similar functions.
It reduces uncertainty.
It produces orientation.
It interprets the invisible.
It structures expectations about the future.

This is precisely why it is so powerful.
Not because it forces people to believe.
But because it increasingly provides the tools with which modern societies perceive reality.

Chapter 10 – The Quantum Revolution

The Dream of Calculating the Future Before It Comes into Being

"Every great fantasy of power in human history has revolved around the same longing: to overcome uncertainty. The quantum computer is the most ambitious attempt yet to transform this longing into technology."

The Next Leap

The history of this book has led us from the priests of Mesopotamia through the financial alchemists of the Renaissance to the algorithms of the present. Every epoch expanded the reach of human prediction.

- Writing stored knowledge.
- Mathematics structured knowledge.
- The computer accelerated knowledge.
- Artificial intelligence automated knowledge.

But now a technology appears that promises to surpass the limits of conventional computing itself. The quantum computer.

For some, it is the next industrial revolution.
For others, an overestimated dream.

For the financial world, however, it represents something even more significant:
The possibility of mastering uncertainty on a new level.

The Limits of the Classical Machine

Every computer of the present is ultimately based on the same basic idea.
Information is represented by bits.
A bit has two states:
0 or 1.

Even the largest data centers in the world consist ultimately of gigantic accumulations of such decisions.
The power of modern systems arises from sheer mass and speed.

Yet certain problems remain extremely difficult.
These include:

- portfolio optimization
- risk analysis
- supply chains
- molecular simulation
- complex prediction models

Not because computers are too slow.
But because the number of possible solutions explodes.
Complexity grows faster than computing power.

The Discovery of Quantum Space

The quantum computer is based on a radically different idea.
Instead of classical bits, it uses qubits.

A qubit can – simplified – represent multiple states simultaneously.
The popular description is:
A qubit can be 0 and 1 at the same time.

Physically, this is only an approximation.
Yet it conveys the central idea:
The quantum computer processes possibilities differently from classical machines.
It does not move linearly through a solution space.
It explores many possibilities simultaneously.

Why the Financial World Is Fascinated

Financial markets are ultimately gigantic systems of possibilities.
Every trade contains:

- different risks,
- different time horizons,
- different probabilities.

The number of possible combinations grows exponentially.

This is precisely where the hope of the financial industry lies.

A quantum computer could theoretically solve problems that classical systems can only approximate.
For example:

- optimal capital allocation,
- complex arbitrage structures,
- dynamic risk distribution,
- market predictions with enormous variable spaces.

The dream is:
Not just calculating faster.
But calculating differently.

The Myth of the Omniscient Computer

At this point, exaggeration often begins.
In popular depictions, the quantum computer appears almost like a technological deity.
An oracle.
A machine that knows every future.

Reality is much more sober.
Quantum computers are not magic.
They do not solve every problem.

They neither replace human thinking nor economic uncertainty.

Many of the most spectacular expectations are based on misunderstandings.
Yet this is precisely why the actual development is more interesting.
Because their power does not lie in omniscience.
But in changing what becomes calculable.

From Speed to Complexity

High-frequency trading conquered time.
The quantum revolution attempts something different.
It conquers complexity.

The decisive competitive advantage in the future may not lie in being the first to receive information.
But in being able to model complex relationships better.

The transition is historically significant.
It marks the shift:
from speed
to structure.
from reaction
to simulation.

from trading
to forecasting.

The Birth of the Quantum Oracle

Here, the quantum revolution touches the central thesis of this book.
Historically, centers of power emerged where uncertainty could be reduced.
The priests interpreted the sky.
The mathematicians calculated probabilities.
The algorithms analyzed data.

The quantum computer promises to potentiate all these abilities.
That is why it appears to many as a modern oracle.
Not because it knows the future.
But because it can evaluate more future possibilities simultaneously.

Reality in the Year 2026

At this point, an important differentiation is necessary.
Public debate often overestimates the current state of development.

In the year 2026, powerful quantum computers and significant research advances do exist.
Yet most financial institutions do not yet work with fully-fledged quantum-based trading systems.

Instead, the following dominate:

- quantum-inspired algorithms,
- hybrid systems,
- optimization methods,
- AI-supported simulations.

The real revolution is currently taking place less in hardware than in thinking.
The financial world is beginning to view problems from a quantum perspective.

The New Geopolitics of Computing

Every transformative technology creates geopolitical competition.
So it was with:

- the steam engine,
- electricity,
- the internet,
- artificial intelligence.

The quantum revolution is no exception.
States are investing billions.

Why?
Because quantum computing promises not only economic advantages.
But strategic power.

Whoever can simulate complex systems better gains advantages in:

- finance,
- logistics,
- materials science,
- cryptography,
- defense.

Control over computing capability becomes a geopolitical resource.

The Threat to Cryptography

A particularly sensitive field concerns the security of digital systems.
Modern encryption relies on mathematical problems that classical computers struggle to solve.

Powerful quantum computers could significantly weaken certain methods.
That is why a global race for so-called post-quantum cryptography is emerging.

The irony is remarkable:
The technology that opens new possibilities simultaneously threatens the foundations of digital trust.

The Financial Elite and the Search for Advantage

Historically, the financial world has always sought informational advantages.
In the past, they were trade routes.
Then telegraphs.
Then computers.
Then high-frequency networks.

The quantum revolution appears as the next logical step.
The incentive is enormous.

Whoever can model uncertainty better possesses:

- better forecasts,
- better risk models,
- better capital allocation.

This gives rise to a new form of economic asymmetry.
Not all market participants possess the same computing power.

The Emergence of Algorithmic Aristocracies

Here one of the central dangers becomes apparent.
Every technological revolution creates winners and losers.
The quantum revolution could amplify this effect.

Because its infrastructure is expensive.
It requires:

- cutting-edge research,
- high technology,
- enormous investments,
- rare expertise.

This creates the possibility of a new knowledge aristocracy.
An elite whose advantage is not based on property alone.
But on exclusive computing capability.

The Philosophical Significance

The deepest significance of the quantum revolution may lie not in the technology itself.
But in the image of humanity that it reveals.

For millennia, humans have tried to reduce uncertainty.

The quantum revolution is an expression of this ancient longing.
It shows the desire:

- to master risks,
- to predict markets,
- to simulate the future,
- to tame complexity.

Yet every expansion of our forecasting ability generates new questions.
If we can see more,
who decides how this knowledge is used?

The Limit of the Predictable

Here we encounter a fundamental truth.
No technology can completely eliminate uncertainty.
Not because computers are too weak.
But because complex systems have principled limits.

Societies.
Markets.
Cultures.
Political orders.
They consist of reflexive actors.
Humans change their behavior as soon as they

know predictions.
This changes the system itself.

The future remains mobile.

The Real Revolution

The quantum revolution therefore does not consist of machines becoming omniscient.
It consists of the boundary between knowledge and non-knowledge shifting.

Some problems become more calculable.
Others only become visible as a result.

Every expansion of our horizon reveals new uncertainties.
This is precisely why the story never ends.
It merely becomes more complex.

Concluding Observation

The quantum computer is neither a savior nor a world ruler.
It is the most advanced tool so far in the long history of human attempts to gain order from uncertainty.

Yet like every powerful technology, it amplifies existing structures.
It amplifies:

- knowledge,
- capital,
- infrastructure,
- power.

The decisive question, therefore, is not:
What can quantum computers do?
But rather:
Who will control them – and for what purpose?

PART III – THE ALGORITMIC PRIESTS

Chapter 11 – The Reign of Possibilities

How Probabilities Begin to Create Reality

"The greatest power is not to predict the future. The greatest power is to create conditions under which a particular future becomes more likely."

The Hidden Turning Point

The history of human power knows a quiet but fundamental transformation.
For a long time, power consisted of reacting to events.
A ruler waited for a crisis.
A general reacted to an attack.
A trader reacted to a market price.

The future appeared as something that was approaching us.
Something that had to be observed, interpreted, and answered.

In the 21st century, this relationship is beginning to reverse.
The new systems no longer merely observe the

future.
They begin to pre-structure it.
They create probability spaces.
And in these spaces, certain developments become more likely than others.

Here begins the reign of possibilities.

The Invisible Power of Probability

Most people understand power as direct intervention.
A command.
A law.
A prohibition.
An instruction.

Yet modern power increasingly acts indirectly.
It does not change the decision itself.
It changes the conditions under which decisions are made.

A simple example:
A supermarket forces no one to buy a particular product.
Yet its placement on the shelf influences the probability of purchase.
The decision remains free.
The probability changes.

This logic becomes the fundamental structure of algorithmic systems.

The Architecture of Decision

Every decision arises within an environment.
This environment determines:

- which information is visible,
- which options appear,
- which risks are perceived,
- which alternatives seem conceivable.

Algorithms shape precisely this environment.
They decide:

- which message appears first,
- which stock is recommended,
- which route is suggested,
- which products become visible.

The user decides.
Yet the architecture of decision has already been shaped.

From the Market of Goods to the Market of Attention

In the industrial age, companies competed for raw materials.
In the information age, they compete for attention.

Attention possesses a remarkable property:
It influences probability.

What receives attention:

- is discussed,
- is invested in,
- is spread,
- is legitimized.

Control over attention thus becomes a form of indirect future-shaping.

The Emergence of the Probabilistic Society

Historical societies organized themselves through rules.
Modern societies increasingly organize themselves through probabilities.

Insurance companies assess risks.
Banks assess default probabilities.
Police systems analyze risk patterns.

Platforms calculate behavioral probabilities.
Markets evaluate future expectations.

Society is no longer primarily steered by prohibitions.
But by predictions.

When Predictions Create Reality

Here we encounter one of the deepest paradoxes of modernity.
A prediction can change people's behavior.
And thereby influence the prediction itself.

An example:
If enough investors believe that a market will rise, they buy.
Through their purchases, the market rises.
The expectation creates reality.

In sociology, this is called a self-fulfilling prophecy.
In the financial world, this is everyday life.

The Reflexivity of Markets

Investor and philosopher George Soros described this mechanism as reflexivity.
People observe the world.
Their observation changes their behavior.
Their changed behavior changes the world.

The world, in turn, influences observation.
A cycle emerges.

Modern algorithms increasingly become part of this cycle.
They observe.
They predict.
They act.
And thereby change the conditions of their own predictions.

The Birth of Synthetic Reality

With increasing digitalization, something new happens.
People no longer react only to physical events.
They react to digital models of reality.

Stock exchanges react to predictions.
Companies react to rankings.
Banks react to ratings.
Politicians react to data analyses.

The representation of reality begins to steer reality itself.
The model becomes part of the system it describes.

The Power of Rankings

Rankings appear harmless.
They order.
Evaluate.
Compare.

Yet rankings change behavior.
When universities are ranked, they change their strategies.
When companies are evaluated, they change their priorities.
When countries are rated, investors react.

The evaluation mechanism itself becomes an actor.
The map begins to influence the territory.

The Market as a Future Machine

Financial markets are the most advanced probability machines in human history.
Every price contains:

- expectations,
- hopes,
- fears,
- predictions.

The market does not evaluate the present.
It evaluates possible futures.

That is why a stock price is never merely a number.
It is a collective statement about probabilities.

The New Power Elite

In the age of possibilities, a new elite emerges.
Not those who control events.
But those who can shape probabilities.

These include:

- operators of large platforms,
- developers of AI systems,
- owners of data infrastructures,
- financial institutions,
- model architects.

Their power does not lie in direct coercion.
It lies in the ability to structure future spaces.

The Financial World as a Laboratory

The financial markets demonstrate this shift particularly clearly.
Algorithms analyze:

- news,
- liquidity,
- market sentiment,
- geopolitical signals,
- social dynamics.

Based on these analyses, capital flows move.
Capital, in turn, changes:

- companies,
- regions,
- technologies,
- states.

The model evaluates the future.
The evaluation influences investments.
Investments change the future.
The loop closes.

The Emergence of Algorithmic Realities

Classical economics assumed that markets reflect reality.
Today, a different dynamic is emerging.
Algorithms are beginning to co-create reality.

When millions of decisions are based on the same models, a new force emerges.
Not the prediction of individual events.
But the generation of collective dynamics.

The market increasingly becomes a self-referential system.

The Illusion of Objectivity

Because models appear mathematical, their results seem objective.
Yet every model contains decisions:

- Which data is used?
- Which factors are weighted?
- Which goals are optimized?
- Which risks are ignored?

The reign of possibilities is therefore never based on neutral probabilities.
It is based on human-defined probability architectures.

The New Form of Sovereignty

Historically, sovereignty meant:
The ability to enact laws.

In the digital age, a new form is emerging.
The ability:

- to control visibility,
- to direct attention,
- to allocate capital,
- to influence probabilities.

Rule shifts from rules to expectations.
From commands to models.
From authority to probability.

The Philosophical Consequence

Here we reach the core of algorithmic esotericism.
Power no longer primarily means:
Forcing people.

Power means:
Structuring possibilities.

Whoever controls the probabilities,
often controls the outcomes,
without ever having to intervene directly.

The future appears open.
Yet its probability landscape has already been shaped.

The Limit of Prediction

Despite all technological progress, a decisive factor remains:
The human being.

Humans are not particles.
Not variables.
Not perfect models.

They possess:

- creativity,
- irrationality,
- resistance,
- capacity for surprise.

Every prediction machine ultimately encounters this limit.
The future remains open because humans remain open.

Concluding Observation

The reign of possibilities is the most subtle form of power that human history has yet produced.
It does not operate through violence.
Not through laws.
Not through open control.

It operates through the shaping of probabilities.
And that is precisely why it often remains invisible.

The decisive political question of the 21st century is therefore not:
Who controls the present?
But rather:
Who shapes the spaces of possible future?

Chapter 12 – Quantum Contracts and Autonomous Markets

The Birth of an Economy That Could Function Without Humans

"Capitalism began as a market between humans. It could end as a market between machines."

The Next Step After the Algorithm

The development of financial markets follows an internal logic.
Each phase attempts to overcome a bottleneck of the previous one.

At first, the human was the bottleneck.
Emotions.
Mistakes.
Slow decisions.

The algorithm replaced many of these weaknesses.
Yet algorithms also have limits.
They require:

- human programming,
- human supervision,
- human contracts,
- human institutions.

The next stage consists of reducing even these dependencies.
Here begins the world of autonomous markets.

From Contracts to Programs

For millennia, a contract was a human instrument.
Two parties made an agreement.
Enforcement occurred through:

- social norms,
- courts,
- states,
- monopolies on violence.

Every contract contained room for interpretation.
Humans could argue.
Judges could weigh.
Contexts could be considered.

The digital revolution fundamentally changes this structure.

The Birth of the Smart Contract

With the development of distributed networks, a new idea emerged.
A contract could be self-executing.
Not as a document.
But as a program.

A so-called smart contract.
It does not merely describe a rule.
It automatically enforces it.

If condition A is met,
then consequence B occurs.
No negotiation.
No interpretation.
No delay.

The contract becomes a machine.

The Path to the Quantum Contract

The term "quantum contract" is deliberately used more broadly in this book than its current technical meaning.
It denotes a new class of agreements:

- highly automated,
- adaptive,
- data-driven,
- algorithmically controlled,
- potentially quantum-optimized.

The quantum contract is no longer merely a document.
It becomes an independent decision-making actor.
It evaluates situations.
It adjusts conditions.
It reacts to market changes.
It develops a limited form of operational autonomy.

The Fusion of Contract and Algorithm

Historically, rules and decisions were separate.
The contract defined the rule.
The human made the decision.

The quantum contract dissolves this separation.
The rule itself becomes the decision-maker.

Thus, a fundamental boundary of civilization shifts.
Humans no longer interpret rules.
Rules begin to execute themselves.

The New Infrastructure of Trust

Trust was long a social resource.
One trusted:

- families,
- communities,
- institutions,
- states.

Digital systems attempt to technically replace trust.
Blockchain systems are an expression of this idea.
Not trust in people.
But trust in protocols.
Not trust in institutions.
But trust in mathematical procedures.

The quantum contract represents the most radical manifestation of this development.

When Capital Speaks with Capital

The classical financial world was based on human communication.
Bankers telephoned.
Traders negotiated.
Investors discussed.

Autonomous markets change this picture.
Machines communicate directly with each other.
Algorithms trade with algorithms.
Liquidity is algorithmically provided.
Risks are algorithmically assessed.

Capital begins to communicate with capital.
The human increasingly disappears from the operational center.

The Emergence of Autonomous Market Actors

One of the most remarkable developments of the present is the emergence of digital actors.
These possess no personality.
No consciousness.
No identity in the human sense.

And yet they make decisions.

Examples include:

- algorithmic trading agents,
- automated liquidity protocols,
- decentralized financial systems,
- self-optimizing investment models.

They act within defined goals.
Yet their concrete decisions arise autonomously.

The Market Without Traders

Since Chapter 4, the figure of the vanished floor trader has accompanied us.
Now this development reaches its logical endpoint.

A market theoretically no longer needs human traders.
It merely needs:

- capital,
- data,
- computing power,
- rules.

Price formation occurs by machine.
Risk analysis occurs by machine.
Execution occurs by machine.

The market becomes a cybernetic structure.

The Emergence of Economic Intelligence

Here begins one of the most fascinating questions of the 21st century.
What happens when millions of algorithms interact simultaneously?

No one controls the overall system.
No one possesses complete overview.
And yet order emerges.

Prices form.
Liquidity distributes.
Risks are absorbed.

The system develops properties that no single actor planned.
This is called emergence.

The Dream of Perfect Efficiency

Proponents of autonomous markets see this as a historic opportunity.

Machines know:

- no fatigue,
- no fear,
- no greed in the human sense,
- no political loyalties.

A fully automated market could theoretically operate:

- more efficiently,
- faster,
- cheaper,
- more stably

than human institutions.
From this perspective, autonomy appears as progress.

The Problem of Goal Setting

Yet every machine pursues goals.
The decisive question, therefore, is:
Who defines these goals?

An algorithm merely optimizes what it was given.
If the goal is:
maximum return
it will maximize return.
Not fairness.
Not social stability.
Not democratic legitimacy.

Autonomy therefore does not solve the power problem.
It shifts it to the level of goal definition.

The New Invisibility

Earlier power structures were visible.
One could recognize:

- the king,
- the bank,
- the government,
- the corporation.

Autonomous systems make this attribution difficult.
Decisions arise from networks.
From protocols.
From models.
From interactions.

Responsibility is distributed across many levels.
Thus, a new form of invisibility emerges.
Not the invisibility of secret rulers.
But the invisibility of complex systems.

Quantum Optimization and Market Coordination

Here the quantum revolution appears once again. Quantum and quantum-inspired methods promise to solve complex coordination problems more efficiently.

For example:

- global capital allocation,
- risk balancing,
- liquidity control,
- network optimization.

Should such systems one day be deployed on a large scale, markets could begin to adapt at a speed and complexity that outruns human observation.
Markets would no longer react.
They would anticipate permanently.

The Danger of Decoupling

However, an autonomous economy harbors a fundamental risk.
Markets do not exist for their own sake.
They are ultimately meant to serve human needs.

If optimization systems pursue exclusively internal efficiency criteria, a decoupling can occur.
The system works technically perfectly.
Yet its results become socially problematic.

Capital flows where models recognize advantages.
Not necessarily where humans have needs.

Here, the motif of algorithmic economic colonialism, already hinted at in the opening text, reappears.

The New Question of Responsibility

Traditional legal systems are based on accountability.
Whoever makes a decision can be held accountable.

But who bears responsibility for an emergent network of autonomous systems?

- The programmer?
- The operator?
- The investor?
- The protocol?
- No one?

This question has no final answer yet.
It could become one of the most important legal debates of the 21st century.

The Metaphysics of Autonomous Markets

On a deeper level, our understanding of the economy is changing.
Classical economics viewed markets as human institutions.

Autonomous markets increasingly appear as independent information ecosystems.
They observe themselves.
They react to themselves.
They optimize themselves.

The economy begins to take on characteristics of a complex organism.
Not conscious.
But self-referential.

The Point of No Return

Every technological revolution has a moment at which it becomes irreversible.
Industrialization reached it with the factory.
Digitalization with the internet.

The algorithmic financial world could reach it with autonomous markets.
From this point onward, human participation would no longer be a prerequisite of the system.
But merely a boundary condition.

Concluding Observation

Quantum contracts and autonomous markets mark the most far-reaching transformation of economic organization to date.
For the first time, the possibility emerges of an economy in which rules are not only set but continuously executed, adapted, and optimized by machines.

The vision is fascinating.
The risks are considerable.

Because every automation of decisions raises the same question:
Who determines the goals that the machines follow?

As long as this question remains unanswered, the future of autonomous markets also remains open

Chapter 13 – Algorithmic Economic Colonialism

How Data, Models, and Capital Create a New Geography of Power

"The colonialism of the 19th century controlled territories. The colonialism of the 21st century controls probabilities."

A New Form of Expansion

When people hear the word colonialism, they think of:

- empires,
- fleets,
- trading companies,
- occupations,
- resource extraction.

They think of visible rule.
Of flags on foreign shores.
Of soldiers and governors.

Yet every era develops its own forms of expansion.
The power of the 21st century rarely moves through armies.
It moves through:

- data,
- algorithms,
- capital flows,
- digital infrastructures,
- platforms.

The new colonialism conquers no countries.
It conquers decision spaces.

The Geography of the Old World

Historical colonialism was based on a simple principle:
Control over resources.

Whoever controlled access to:

- gold,
- silver,
- spices,
- oil,
- trade routes

controlled wealth.
Power was geographical.
It depended on territories.
That is why maps became instruments of rule.
Empires drew borders.
And borders determined wealth.

The Geography of the Data World

In the information age, the map shifts.
The most valuable resources are no longer primarily underground.
They arise from human behavior.

Every click.
Every movement.

Every purchase.
Every search query.
Every digital interaction.

This information becomes raw material.
Not because it is valuable in isolation.
But because, in gigantic quantities, it reveals patterns.

Data becomes the new ore of the digital age.

The New Extraction

Historical empires extracted raw materials.
Modern platforms extract information.

The mechanism shows astonishing parallels.
In the past, raw materials left the colony.
Today, data leaves the user.

In both cases, value is created through processing elsewhere.
The actual value creation does not occur where the resource originates.
But where it is analyzed, combined, and monetized.

The Invisible Raw Material Economy

Most people do not realize that they produce data daily.
They experience:

- communication,
- entertainment,
- navigation,
- consumption.

Yet in the background, gigantic datasets are created.
These datasets enable:

- behavioral predictions,
- risk models,
- market analyses,
- AI training,
- political influence.

The raw material is supplied voluntarily.
Often without conscious awareness of its value.

The Birth of the Model Empires

Historical empires controlled territories.
The new empires control models.

A model possesses an extraordinary property.
It can be applied to millions or billions of people.
A successful algorithm scales almost without limit.

Thus, a form of power emerges that transcends geographical boundaries.
The model travels.
The infrastructure remains.
The impact globalizes.

The Financial Markets as Amplifiers

Nowhere is this mechanism more evident than in the global financial system.
Modern capital flows increasingly follow algorithmic assessments.

Models analyze:

- stability,
- risk,
- growth,
- liquidity,
- geopolitical signals.

Then investments move.
Not because of personal relationships.
Not because of cultural proximity.
But because of mathematical attractiveness.

When Models Evaluate Countries

Here the real transformation begins.
A state is increasingly viewed not primarily as a political community.
But as a dataset.
As a bundle of variables.

For example:

- inflation rates,
- debt levels,
- demographics,
- energy prices,
- political stability.

From these variables, evaluations emerge.
From evaluations, capital flows emerge.
And from capital flows, real economic consequences emerge.

The Power of Risk Models

Risk appears as an objective category.
In reality, it is an interpretation.

Every risk model contains assumptions.
These assumptions influence:

- investments,
- lending,
- interest rates,
- access to capital.

A country may appear economically healthy.
Yet if models perceive risks, capital flows away.
The model itself becomes a geopolitical actor.

The New Periphery

In classical colonialism, centers and peripheries existed.
Raw materials moved from the periphery to the center.
Value creation concentrated in the center.

In the digital age, a similar pattern emerges.
Data arises everywhere.
Yet its processing concentrates in a few regions.

There, one finds:

•data centers,
•research laboratories,
•financial centers,
•AI infrastructures.

The digital periphery supplies raw material.
The digital centers create value.

The Algorithm as Governor

The historical governor represented the empire locally.
The algorithm today fulfills a comparable function.

It decides:

•which content becomes visible,
•which companies are financed,
•which markets appear attractive,
•which risks seem acceptable.

These decisions are not political in their making.
Yet their effects are political.

The algorithm manages attention, capital, and visibility.

The Emergence of Asymmetric Reality

A central feature of algorithmic systems is their asymmetry.
The evaluated usually do not see the models.
The modelers see the evaluated very precisely.

This creates a power imbalance.
Historically, the colonial administrator possessed maps, surveys, and statistics.
The local population rarely had access to the same information.

Today, a similar information asymmetry arises.
The platform knows the user better than the user knows the platform.

The Reign of Correlation

Another feature of algorithmic economic colonialism is that decisions are increasingly based on correlations.
Not on cultural understanding.
Not on historical contexts.
Not on human experience.
But on patterns.

A model does not ask:
Why does this problem exist?
It asks:
Which variables correlate with this problem?

This shift changes the logic of economic decisions.

Capital as an Autonomous Flow

In the early chapters of this book, we encountered the idea of autonomous markets.
Here, its geopolitical consequence becomes apparent.

Capital begins to behave like an intelligent flow.
It seeks:

- efficiency,
- returns,
- stability,
- pattern quality.

It does not move based on moral criteria.
It follows algorithmic logic.

Thus, winners and losers emerge without any single actor consciously intending it.

The New Form of Dependency

Historical colonies became dependent on external powers.

The digital world creates new dependencies.
On:

- cloud infrastructures,
- payment networks,
- platform economies,
- AI systems,
- data architectures.

These dependencies are less visible than military control.
Yet they can be equally profound.

The Illusion of Neutrality

Proponents of algorithmic systems often emphasize their neutrality.
The algorithm does not discriminate.
It merely calculates.

Yet models are never completely neutral.
They reflect:

- data,
- goals,
- weightings,
- assumptions.

Every such decision has political and economic consequences.

The neutrality of the machine can therefore easily become the invisibility of power.

The New Extractivism

Historical empires extracted raw materials.
Algorithmic economic colonialism extracts something else:
Behavior.
Attention.
Predictability.

The actual raw material is no longer matter.
It is the human future.
Because every model ultimately attempts to make future behavior calculable.

The Counter-Movements

Like every power structure, this new order also generates resistance.
Worldwide, demands are emerging for:

- data sovereignty,
- algorithmic transparency,
- digital self-determination,
- local infrastructure,
- public AI research.

These movements understand that the decisive conflicts of the future will be fought less over territories than over information spaces.

The Deeper Meaning

The term "algorithmic economic colonialism" should not be understood as a simple accusation.
It describes a structure.
A dynamic.
A shift of power.

The central question is not whether individual actors have evil intentions.
The central question is:
What consequences arise when global systems organize capital and attention according to criteria that only a few understand and control?

Concluding Observation

The colonialism of the industrial age controlled land.
Algorithmic economic colonialism controls models.

It does not occupy territories.
It occupies probability spaces.

It does not directly determine what happens.
It influences what is likely to happen.

Thus, a form of power emerges that is more subtle, more global, and often more invisible than its historical predecessors.
The great conflicts of the future will therefore be fought not only over resources.
But over data.
Over models.
Over computing power.
And over the question of who controls the architecture of probability.

Chapter 14 – The New Aristocracy

The Owners of Probabilities

"In every era, there exists a class that not only possesses wealth but determines the rules by which wealth is created. The aristocracy of the information age owns no lands. It owns models."

The End of the Old Elites?

Modernity long believed in a grand narrative:
That technological progress would dissolve old hierarchies.
Democracy was supposed to limit the power of kings.

Capitalism was supposed to replace the power of the nobility.
Education was supposed to overcome birth.
Digitalization was supposed to democratize knowledge.

And indeed, many traditional power structures were weakened.
Yet history knows no power vacuum.
When one elite disappears, another usually emerges.

The question, therefore, is not:
Do elites exist?
But rather:
Who forms the elite of any given era?

The Aristocracy of Land

In the Middle Ages, power was based on land.
Land meant:

- food,
- taxes,
- soldiers,
- political control.

The nobility did not possess power because they were smarter.

But because they controlled the most important resource of their time.

The aristocratic order was ultimately an infrastructure order.
Whoever controlled land controlled society.

The Aristocracy of Capital

With industrialization, power shifted.
Factories became more important than fields.
Capital became more important than land.

A new elite emerged:

- industrialists,
- bankers,
- financial dynasties,
- entrepreneurs.

They controlled the means of production.
The possession of capital replaced the possession of land.

The logic remained the same.
The central resource determines the ruling class.

The Aristocracy of Information

In the information age, power shifts once again.
The decisive resource is no longer primarily:

- land,
- factories,
- machines.

But rather:

- data,
- models,
- networks,
- computing power,
- attention.

Whoever controls these resources gains a structural advantage.
Not only economically.
But socially and politically.

The Birth of the Model Owners

In the previous chapters, we have seen:

- data generates models,
- models generate predictions,
- predictions influence decisions,
- decisions change reality.

From this, a new concentration of power follows.
The decisive actors are no longer merely capital owners.

They are owners of prediction machines.
Owners of probability architectures.
Owners of algorithmic reality.

The New Form of Property

Historically, property was visible.
A castle.
A mine.
A factory.
A plot of land.

The new aristocracy often owns intangible assets.
For example:

- training data,
- algorithms,
- platforms,
- AI models,
- network effects.

These goods possess an extraordinary property.
They become more valuable the more people use them.
Thus, self-reinforcing power structures emerge.

The Mathematics of Concentration

The wealth of the new aristocracy does not grow linearly.
It grows exponentially.

Why?
Because digital systems possess economies of scale.
A model can serve:

- a hundred people,
- a thousand people,
- a billion people.

Costs increase only to a limited extent.
The impact grows enormously.

Thus, a concentration emerges that earlier economic systems hardly knew.

The Owners of Infrastructure

One of the most important insights of this book is:
Power rarely lies on the surface.
It lies in the infrastructure.

The new aristocracy often does not control the visible market.
It controls the infrastructure of the market.

This includes:

- cloud systems,
- AI platforms,
- payment networks,
- data centers,
- chip production,
- trading architectures.

Whoever controls infrastructure controls possibilities.

The New Heredity

Aristocracies are historically characterized by inheritance.
Privileges are passed on.

Interestingly, a similar dynamic emerges in the digital age.
Not through titles.
Not through patents of nobility.
But through access.

Access to:

- education,
- data,
- capital,
- networks,
- technology.

The children of the new elite grow up within an ecosystem that gives them structural advantages.
The form changes.
The function remains familiar.

The Knowledge Aristocracy

The new elite not only possesses wealth.
It also possesses knowledge.
Or more precisely:
It possesses access to knowledge systems.

The most important resources of the 21st century are highly complex.
Only a few people understand:

- AI architectures,
- quantum optimization,
- financial models,
- global data networks.

Thus, a knowledge asymmetry emerges.
This asymmetry becomes the foundation of new power.

The New Legitimation

Every aristocracy needs a justification.
The nobility invoked birth.
The industrial elite invoked entrepreneurial spirit.
The new aristocracy invokes competence.

It argues:
We control these systems because we understand them.

This claim is not completely false.
The complexity of modern systems requires expertise.
Yet expertise alone does not answer the question of legitimacy.

The Invisibility of the New Nobility

Historical aristocrats were visible.
They lived in palaces.
Wore titles.
Held public offices.

The new aristocracy is harder to recognize.
Its power operates through:

- ownership structures,
- shareholdings,
- platforms,
- data flows,
- model architectures.

Often it remains in the background.
Precisely for that reason, it is rarely perceived as an aristocracy.

The Rise of the Techno-Feudal Order

Some political thinkers today use the term "techno-feudalism."
It refers to the idea that digital platforms fulfill similar functions as feudal lords once did.

The analogy is not perfect.
Yet it points to something important.

Many people move within digital territories that do not belong to them.
They work.
Communicate.
Trade.
Consume.

Yet the infrastructure belongs to others.

The Financial Aristocracy of the Future

This development becomes particularly evident in high finance.

Whoever in the future possesses:

- quantum optimization,
- AI-supported predictions,
- global data sources,
- autonomous trading systems,

possesses a structural advantage.
This advantage generates:

- higher profits,
- better data,
- better models,
- even higher profits.

A cycle emerges.
The aristocracy reproduces itself.

The Danger of a Closed Elite

Every elite faces the same temptation.
To insulate itself.
To secure its advantages.
To limit access.
To reduce competition.

When the new aristocracy begins to control knowledge, infrastructure, and capital simultaneously, a risk arises.
Not necessarily tyranny.
But ossification.

Social dynamics depend on new actors being able to rise.

The Countervailing Forces

History never runs one-sidedly.
Every concentration of power is followed by counter-movements.

In the digital age, these could arise through:

- open-source initiatives,
- public research,
- decentralized networks,
- algorithmic transparency,
- digital fundamental rights.

These forces attempt to make the infrastructure of the future more broadly accessible.

The Real Question

The existence of an elite is historically nothing new.
What is new is the nature of its power.

The new aristocracy does not primarily control people.
It controls:

- information flows,
- models,
- probabilities,
- attention,
- digital infrastructure.

Thus, it controls the conditions under which decisions arise.

Concluding Observation

The aristocracy of the 21st century wears no crowns.
It bears no coats of arms.
It rarely rules through direct commands.

Its power lies deeper.
It owns the systems that determine what becomes visible.
It owns the models that assess risks.

It owns the infrastructure on which markets, communication, and knowledge are based.

It is not a return of the old nobility.
It is its algorithmic mutation.

An aristocracy of data.
An aristocracy of models.
An aristocracy of probability.

Chapter 15 – The Fragility of the Perfect Machine

Why the Most Powerful Systems in History Might Also Be the Most Vulnerable

"The more perfect a system becomes, the less room it has for surprises. And that is precisely where catastrophe waits."

The Dream of Perfect Order

Since the beginning of civilization, humanity has pursued an ancient dream.
The creation of a perfect order.
An order without:

- chaos,

- uncertainty,
- error,
- waste,
- crises.

The priests wanted to appease the gods.
The kings wanted stable empires.
The bureaucracies wanted calculable administration.
The economists wanted efficient markets.
The computer scientists want optimal systems.

Again and again, the same vision appears:
If we gather enough knowledge, we can master the world.

The Fulfillment of the Ancient Dream

In the algorithmic age, this dream seems more tangible than ever.
We possess:

- global data networks,
- artificial intelligence,
- quantum optimization,
- autonomous markets,
- real-time analyses.

Never before could a civilization observe itself to such an extent.

Never before could it model its processes so precisely.
Never before could it make decisions so quickly.

And this is precisely where the paradox begins.

Why Perfect Systems Break

Complex systems rarely fail because of their weaknesses.
They often fail because of their strengths.

A system is optimized.
Further and further.
More and more precisely.
More and more efficiently.
Until every reserve disappears.
Until every redundancy appears as waste.
Until every delay is eliminated.

Then a small shock is enough.
And the system reacts disproportionately.

The Lesson of Nature

Nature does not work according to maximum efficiency.
It works according to resilience.

Forests possess:

- overlaps,
- redundancies,
- diversity,
- seemingly inefficient structures.

These properties seem wasteful.
Yet they ensure survival.

A forest survives storms because it is not perfectly optimized.
It possesses leeway.

The Logic of the Machine

Algorithms think differently.
They seek:

- minimization,
- optimization,
- efficiency,
- speed.

What is not needed is removed.
What causes costs is reduced.
What is slow is accelerated.

Within narrow parameters, this produces impressive results.
Yet in the long term, the same logic can generate fragility.

The Financial World as a Warning Sign

Modern financial history provides numerous examples.
Before every major crisis, there existed a widespread belief:
The system has become more stable.

Before 1987.
Before 1998.
Before 2008.
Before numerous flash crashes.

Again and again, experts believed they had better understood risks.
And again and again, new risks emerged in unexpected places.
Not despite the models.
But partly because of them.

The Illusion of Control

The more data becomes available, the more the illusion of control grows.
People begin to believe:

- Everything is measurable.
- Everything is modelable.
- Everything is predictable.

Yet models not only generate knowledge.
They also generate overconfidence.
And excessive overconfidence is among the most dangerous forces of complex systems.

The Homogenization of Thinking

One of the greatest dangers of algorithmic systems lies in their homogenization.

When millions of market participants use the same models,
they see the same signals.
Assess the same risks.
Make similar decisions.

In the short term, stability emerges.
In the long term, vulnerability emerges.
Because diversity disappears.

The Catastrophe of Synchronization

Historical markets consisted of diverse actors.
People reacted differently.
At different speeds.
With different beliefs.

Modern systems synchronize behavior.
When many algorithms react simultaneously,
feedback loops arise.
A small movement is amplified.

An amplification generates further reactions.
A cycle emerges.

The result can be extreme market movements.

The Quantum Flash Crash

In the opening text of this book, the possibility of so-called quantum flash crashes was described. Whether this term becomes technically established in the future or not, it points to a real concern.

The more complex and faster systems become, the shorter the time between cause and effect. Human intervention becomes increasingly impossible.

The market reacts faster than humans can even recognize what is happening.

The Tyranny of Optimization

Every optimization has a goal.
And that is precisely where its problem lies.

Because the world never pursues only one goal.
A financial system must simultaneously be:

- efficient,
- stable,

•fair,
•innovative,
•resilient.

If one optimizes exclusively for efficiency,
other properties are weakened.

The perfect machine can therefore destroy its own foundation.

The Black Swan

Essayist and risk theorist Nassim Nicholas Taleb coined the concept of the "Black Swan."
It refers to events

•that are rare,
•appear difficult to predict,
•have enormous consequences.

The greatest weakness of many models is that they are based on known patterns.
Yet the Black Swan lives outside the known patterns.

That is precisely where the power of prediction ends.

The Return of the Unknown

The algorithmic age attempts to reduce uncertainty.
Yet uncertainty does not disappear.
It shifts.

When known risks are better controlled,
unknown risks emerge more strongly.

The history of complex systems shows:
Every solved uncertainty generates new uncertainties.
The boundary of knowledge shifts.
It does not disappear.

Emergence as a Blind Spot

The most dangerous developments often arise not from errors.
But from interactions.

A single algorithm can work completely correctly.
Thousands of correctly working algorithms can nevertheless jointly generate instability.

Here we encounter the principle of emergence.
The overall system develops properties
that were contained in none of its individual parts.
No one planned them.
No one controls them completely.
And yet they arise.

The Vulnerability of Infrastructure

The new aristocracy controls:

- data,
- models,
- networks,
- data centers.

Yet precisely this concentration generates vulnerability.
The more central a system becomes,
the greater the consequences of its failure.

A single node can have effects on:

- markets,
- communication,
- supply chains,
- financial systems.

The strength of networking becomes the source of new risks.

The Human Variable

In all future scenarios of this book, the same limit appears again and again.
The human being.

Humans do not act completely rationally.
They surprise.
They contradict expectations.
They change rules.
They rebel.

From the perspective of many models, these properties appear as disturbances.
In truth, they often form the most important source of societal adaptability.

The Illusion of Infallibility

Every power order eventually develops the belief in its own stability.
Empires believed in their eternity.
Monarchies believed in their legitimacy.
Ideologies believed in their truth.

Algorithmic systems can also succumb to this temptation.
The conviction:
The model knows better.

Yet that is precisely where the danger begins.
Not in the technology.
But in the belief in its infallibility.

The Wisdom of Imperfection

Perhaps the most important lesson of complex systems lies in a surprising insight:
Perfection is not always an advantage.

Some errors are useful.
Some detours are valuable.
Some inefficiencies create resilience.

Nature has learned this over billions of years.
Digital civilization is only beginning to understand this lesson.

The Philosophical Consequence

The greatest challenge of the 21st century may not be to build better models.
But to accept limits.

To recognize that:

- knowledge remains limited,
- predictions remain uncertain,
- systems remain capable of being surprised.

The future can be influenced.
But never completely owned.

Concluding Observation

The perfect machine is the great promise of the algorithmic age.
A system
that sees everything,
calculates everything,
optimizes everything.

Yet this very vision contains its own contradiction.
Because the more comprehensive the optimization,
the greater the danger
that the system loses its ability to deal with the unexpected.

The future, therefore, likely belongs not to the most perfect systems.
But to the most resilient ones.
Not to the fastest.
But to the most adaptable.
Not to the omniscient machines.
But to those societies that have learned to live with uncertainty.

Chapter 16 – The Great Decoupling

When Markets, Machines, and Humans No Longer Follow the Same Reality

"The greatest revolution does not happen when machines become smarter. It happens when their logic begins to detach itself from human logic."

The Moment of Separation

Every civilization rests on a fundamental assumption:
That its central institutions ultimately serve the needs of humans.
Markets exist to distribute goods.
Banks exist to provide capital.
Governments exist to organize societies.
Technologies exist to expand human capabilities.

But what happens when this connection weakens?
When systems continue to function –
but it becomes increasingly difficult to comprehend whom they actually serve?

Here begins the great decoupling.

The Historical Unity

For millennia, economy and society were closely intertwined.
A farmer produced food.
A craftsman made tools.
A merchant traded goods.

The connection between work, value, and wealth was visible.
Not always just.
Not always efficient.
But fundamentally understandable.

People could recognize how economic activity was connected to their lives.

The First Decoupling: Financial Capital

With industrialization, the first major distancing began.
Capital became increasingly abstract.
Stocks.
Bonds.
Derivatives.
Financial products.

Wealth was no longer exclusively tied to physical production.
The financial world developed its own dynamics.

Nevertheless, it remained ultimately connected to the real economy.
Factories continued to produce real goods.

The Second Decoupling: Digitalization

The digital revolution accelerated this process.
Value increasingly arose through:

- software,
- networks,
- data,
- platforms,
- attention.

A company could be worth billions without owning large physical assets.
The connection between material production and market valuation became weaker.
The market began to value expectations higher than present reality.

The Third Decoupling: Algorithmization

With the rise of algorithmic systems, a new stage emerges.
Machines do not act based on human narratives.
They act based on:

- patterns,
- probabilities,
- correlations,
- optimization functions.

For an algorithm, a story has no meaning.
A nation has no identity.
A tradition has no intrinsic value.
Only data points exist.

The language of markets begins to detach itself from the language of humans.

Two Realities Emerge

The modern world increasingly develops two parallel realities.

The human reality
It consists of:

- experiences,
- hopes,
- fears,
- identities,
- cultural meanings.

The algorithmic reality
It consists of:

- datasets,
- probabilities,
- optimization functions,
- models,
- correlations.

For a long time, both worlds overlapped.
Today, they are drifting apart.

The Market Does Not Understand Stories

Humans think in stories.
Machines think in patterns.

A society tells itself:
We are investing in our future.
A model records:
Expected return: 3.7%.

A country describes itself as a cultural community.
An algorithm assesses:
Risk profile elevated.

Here a fundamental difference arises.
The machine reduces meaning to calculability.

The Decoupling of Capital

Today, capital moves with a speed and flexibility that historical societies never knew.
Within seconds, it can:

- leave markets,
- change currencies,
- redistribute risks,
- leap across continents.

Humans, by contrast, remain:

- local,
- culturally embedded,
- institutionally bound.

Capital becomes global.
Humans remain physical.
The interests of the two begin to diverge.

The Decoupling of Labor

Another dimension becomes apparent in the world of work.
Traditionally, income arose from participation in value creation.

The digital economy is changing this relationship.
Ever larger values arise through:

•automation,
•scaling,
•platform effects,
•AI systems.

Productivity grows.
Yet not necessarily societal participation.
Wealth and work are moving away from each other.

The Decoupling of Information

In earlier societies, information was scarce.
Today, it is superabundant.

Paradoxically, this does not create a shared reality.
But many parallel realities.

Algorithms personalize information.
Everyone sees a different world.
Everyone receives different signals.

This makes collective understanding more difficult.
Society loses its common information base.

The Decoupling of Responsibility

Historical decisions had identifiable authors.
A king decided.
A parliament resolved.
A board approved.

Algorithmic systems blur this attribution.
Decisions arise from:

- models,
- datasets,
- optimization processes,
- networks.

Responsibility becomes diffuse.
The action remains visible.
The actor disappears.

The Decoupling of Democracy

Democracy is based on a simple principle:
People should have influence over the forces that determine their lives.

Yet many decisive systems increasingly lie outside classical democratic control.
For example:

- global capital flows,
- platform architectures,
- AI models,

•financial algorithms.

The political sphere loses influence over processes that deeply intervene in society.
This creates tensions.

The Decoupling of Time

Humans live in biological time.
Markets live in algorithmic time.

A human thinks in:

•days,
•months,
•years.

An algorithm operates in:

•milliseconds,
•microseconds,
•nanoseconds.

The timeframes begin to differ.
What is present for humans already appears as past to machines.

The Decoupling of Knowledge

Modern systems become increasingly complex.
Only a few specialists understand their architecture.

Thus, a new divide emerges.
The majority uses systems.
A minority understands them.

This knowledge asymmetry recalls earlier eras:

- priests understood rituals,
- scholars understood scriptures,
- experts understand algorithms.

The knowledge order becomes hierarchical once again.

The Psychological Consequence

Many people intuitively feel the great decoupling.
They experience:

- economic uncertainty,
- institutional distrust,
- technological overwhelm.

Yet often the language to describe these experiences is lacking.

The feeling is:
The world is being moved by forces that I can neither see nor influence.

This very feeling forms the emotional core of algorithmic esotericism.

The Return of the Mythological

Paradoxically, extreme rationalization often leads to new myths.
When systems become too complex, narratives emerge.
Conspiracies.
Promises of salvation.
Technological religions.

People seek meaning where transparency is lacking.
The black box becomes the modern chamber of mysteries.

The Question of the Human Role

The great decoupling ultimately poses an existential question.
What role does the human play in an order

increasingly analyzed, optimized, and controlled by machines?

Is he:

- user?
- owner?
- raw material supplier?
- decision-maker?
- observer?

The answer is still open.

The Possibility of Recoupling

Decoupling is not a natural law.
It is the result of decisions.

Societies can create new connections:

- democratic control,
- algorithmic transparency,
- public research,
- digital education,
- institutional reforms.

The question is not whether technology should exist.
The question is how it is embedded into human goals.

The Deeper Meaning

The great decoupling does not describe the victory of the machine over humans.
It describes a growing distance between different logics.

Between:

- meaning and calculation,
- culture and optimization,
- experience and data,
- human and model.

The greater this distance becomes,
the greater the challenge for modern societies.

Concluding Observation

The algorithmic revolution is not only changing markets.
It is changing the relationship between humans and reality.

For the first time, the possibility arises that the most important systems of our civilization operate according to rules that are effective but no longer intuitively understandable.

Thus, the central political task of the 21st century becomes visible:
Not the prevention of technological progress.
But the restoration of a connection between human values and machine power.

For a society can only remain permanently stable if its people understand why the world works the way it works.

Chapter 17 – The Constitution of Algorithms

Who Writes Rules When Rules Themselves Act

"In the past, laws limited people. Today, laws must limit systems that are faster than any institution."

The Moment When Law Is No Longer Enough

Legal systems are among the oldest technologies of humanity.
They are based on a simple assumption:
That actions are comprehensible.

A law describes:

- what is permitted,
- what is forbidden,
- what happens in case of conflict.

Yet this structure presupposes something:
Time.
Time for interpretation.
Time for proceedings.
Time for objection.

Algorithmic systems reduce precisely this time.
They act in milliseconds.
They react in real time.
And they change states before a legal process can even begin.

The Classical Constitution of the World

Modern democracy is based on constitutions.
A constitution is not a law in the narrow sense.
It is a framework.

It defines:

- fundamental rights,
- limitation of power,
- institutional balance,
- separation of powers.

It is slow.
Intentionally slow.
Because stability arises through delay.

The New Question: What Is a Constitution for Machines?

When systems begin to act autonomously,
a new question arises:
Which rules apply to actors that are not human?

An algorithm knows no morality.
No intention.
No responsibility in the classical sense.
It optimizes.
Always.
Continuously.
Without pause.

The Emergence of Implicit Constitutions

In today's digital world, "invisible constitutions" already exist.
They are not codified in a single document.
They arise from:

- platform rules,
- API structures,
- training data,
- security protocols,
- regulatory frameworks,
- economic incentives.

These elements collectively determine what systems may do and what they will effectively do. Yet no one designed them as a whole.

Code as Law

A central shift of recent decades is:
Code increasingly replaces rulebooks.

When a smart contract is executed, it is not:
"The court will decide later."
But rather:
"The code decides immediately."

Thus, law shifts from:
interpretation → execution

An implemented algorithm is not merely a proposal.
It is action.

The Irreversibility of Digital Rules

A classical law can be changed.
A court can interpret it.
A parliament can reform it.

An algorithmic system is often harder to change.
Why?

- Systems are networked.
- Changes have cascade effects.
- Updates require coordination.
- Errors can have global consequences.

Thus, a new form of institutional inertia emerges.
Not through bureaucracy.
But through technical complexity.

The Constitution of Platforms

Large digital platforms already possess constitution-like structures today.
They define:

- visibility (ranking algorithms),
- terms of participation (usage rules),
- economic participation (monetization),
- sanctions (deplatforming, bans).

These rules function like laws.
Yet they are designed privately.
And changed at any time.

The Algorithmic Separation of Powers

In classical democracies, there is a separation of powers:

- legislative (laws),
- executive (execution),
- judicial (interpretation).

In algorithmic systems, these functions blur.
A system can simultaneously:

- define rules (through optimization),
- apply them (through execution),
- and "interpret" them (through model adaptation).

The separation of powers becomes technically fuzzy.

The Necessity of New Control Bodies

When systems become more autonomous,
a new category of institutions emerges:

- algorithmic supervisory authorities,
- model auditors,
- data ethics councils,
- AI compliance systems.

Their task would be not only control.
But translation:
Between human norms and machine logic.

The Idea of an Algorithmic Constitution

A possible answer to the emerging complexity is the idea of a "constitution of algorithms."
It would not be a single document.
But a system of principles such as:

- transparency obligations for critical models,
- traceability of decisions,
- limitation of optimization goals,
- obligation to enable human intervention,
- documentation of training data sources,
- audit mechanisms for systemic risks.

Yet these principles must be implemented technically.
Not merely formulated legally.

The Problem of Translation

Law is linguistic.
Algorithms are mathematical.
Between them lies a gap.

When a law says:
"Discrimination is prohibited."
a system must define:

- What is discrimination in data?
- How is it measured?

- Which thresholds apply?
- Which variables are relevant?

Every translation changes the content.
Thus, a new field of power emerges:
The interpretation of norms in code.

The Invisible Legislation

In the algorithmic world, rules often arise without democratic debate.
Through:

- technical standards,
- corporate decisions,
- model architectures,
- market incentives.

These processes appear neutral.
But they are not.
Because every architecture implicitly decides on:

- access,
- visibility,
- participation,
- risk,
- opportunities.

The Question of Legitimacy

In classical states, the principle is:
Laws are legitimate if they were democratically decided.

But what legitimizes an algorithm?

- Its efficiency?
- Its accuracy?
- Its economic impact?
- Its technical superiority?

Or should new criteria exist?
This question is unresolved.
And it will become central to the future of political systems.

The Limits of Control

Even if a constitution for algorithms existed,
one problem would remain:
Complexity.

The more complex systems become,
the more difficult complete control becomes.
Even developers often no longer understand all the emergent properties of their models.
Thus, the constitution encounters a moving target.

The Danger of Pseudo-Control

A particularly risky scenario arises when control is only simulated.
For example:

- audit reports without depth,
- compliance as a formality,
- transparency as marketing,
- ethics as a PR tool.

Then an illusion of security emerges.
While actual complexity continues to grow.

The Geopolitical Dimension

The question of the algorithmic constitution is not only technical.
It is geopolitical.

Countries and regions compete for:

- AI infrastructure,
- data access,
- computing power,
- model leadership.

Whoever determines the rules of the systems, indirectly determines global power relations.

The Return of the Concept of Sovereignty

At its core, it is about an old question:
Who is sovereign?

In the past, it was the king.
Then the state.
Then the market.

Today, a new possibility arises:
That sovereignty partly passes to systems
that are neither clearly state-owned nor private.

The Constitution as a Living System

One possible future vision is a "dynamic constitution."
It would not be a static document,
but an adaptive system:

- continuously reviewed,
- algorithmically monitored,
- human-corrected,
- institutionally embedded.

It would attempt
to connect the speed of machines
with the slowness of democracy.

Concluding Observation

The constitution of algorithms is not a marginal legal issue.
It is the central political challenge of a world in which decisions are increasingly made by non-human systems.

The decisive shift is:
No longer only humans need protection from power.
But humans also need protection from the logic of their own systems.

For every technology
that makes decisions
already carries a form of constitution within itself.
The only question is:
Who wrote it?

Chapter 18 – Beyond Algorithmic Esotericism

When Machines No Longer Seem Mystical But Become Matter-of-Fact

"The secret does not disappear when we understand it. It disappears when we stop treating it as a secret."

The End of Esotericism

The term "algorithmic esotericism" arose in this book from an observation:
The more complex systems become, the more they begin to appear mystical to humans.

- Markets move without recognizable cause.
- Capital flows seemingly "intelligently."
- Models decide without explainable logic.
- Systems react faster than human perception.

What is not understood is often interpreted mythically.
Yet here lies a decisive turning point:
Esotericism is not a state of the systems.
It is a state of perception.

The Disenchantment of the Black Box

In the previous chapters, the world appeared increasingly opaque:

- quantum contracts,
- autonomous markets,
- algorithmic aristocracies,
- decoupled realities,
- constitutions of machines.

All this created the impression of a "second reality" behind the visible world.
Yet this second reality is not hidden.
It is merely distributed.

Complexity Is Not a Mystery

A central error of modern perception is:
"Complex = mysterious."

In fact:
Complexity is often explainable – but not intuitively graspable.

A weather model is not a mystery.
A neural network is not an oracle.
A financial system is not a conscious entity.

They are:

- systems of many interactions,
- feedback loops,
- statistical processes,
- optimizing structures.

The feeling of the mystical arises where human intuition ends.
Not where truth is hidden.

The Third Phase: Normalization of AI

Every technological revolution goes through three phases:

1.Shock
"This is incomprehensible."
2.Mythologization
"This is superhuman."
3.Normalization
"This is infrastructure."

Electricity was once magical.
The internet was once revolutionary.

AI and algorithmic financial systems are currently between phases 2 and 3.
This book has deliberately made visible the phase of mythologization.
Now its dissolution begins.

The Return of Mechanics

When systems are fully integrated, they disappear from consciousness.
No one thinks about power grids when turning on a light.
No one thinks about routing protocols when sending a message.

No one thinks about market infrastructure when trading.

The same will happen with algorithmic systems.
They will not disappear.
They will become invisible.
Because they work.

The Dissolution of "Invisible Forces"

The opening text of this book spoke of:
invisible forces that direct global financial flows

Yet after the journey through the chapters, it becomes clear:
These forces are not invisible because they are hidden.
But because they are distributed:

- in data centers,
- in models,
- in market structures,
- in regulatory systems,
- in human behavior.

There is no center of control.
There are only networks of decisions.

The End of the "Quantum Myth"

The term "quantum trading" also seemed like a transition into the mystical in the opening text.
Yet reality is less metaphysical:

- quantum computing is experimental,
- many "quantum-inspired" methods are classical optimizations,
- the real revolution lies in data, scaling, and speed.

The seemingly "supernatural" is often merely:
a conventional technology in extreme dimensions.

The True Transformation: Speed + Scaling

The real revolution of financial and AI systems is not their mysteriousness.
But rather:

- speed,
- parallelism,
- data volume,
- networking.

When a system reacts faster than human perception,
it automatically appears as "no longer human."
Yet this is an epistemic illusion.

The Human as Interpretation Machine

Humans tend to personalize causes.
When something works, we ask:

- Who is behind it?
- Who controls it?
- Who benefits?

Yet many modern systems have no central intention.
They arise from:

- local optimizations,
- decentralized decisions,
- emergent effects.

The result appears intentional.
But it is not necessarily so.

The Demystification of Power

A central conclusion of this book is:
The new power is not secret.
It is structural.

It consists of:

- architectural decisions,
- data access,

- model parameters,
- infrastructure control,
- feedback dynamics.

Whoever understands these structures recognizes:
There is no "hidden controller."
There are only different levels of influence.

The New Competence: Systems Thinking

In a world of algorithmic systems, the most important skill shifts:
No longer intuition about individual events.
But understanding of systems.

Whoever wants to understand the world must learn:

- to recognize feedback loops,
- to analyze incentive systems,
- to read data flows,
- to question model assumptions,
- to understand economies of scale.

Systems thinking replaces mystery.

The New Responsibility

When systems become explainable, responsibility does not disappear.
On the contrary:
It becomes more concrete.

Because then it becomes visible:

- which decisions were made,
- which parameters were chosen,
- which goals are being optimized,
- which risks were accepted.

Transparency is not a technical question.
It is a political decision.

The Last Illusion: Control

One of the central themes of this book was the question of control.
Yet in the end, it becomes clear:
Control was never absolute.
Neither in human systems.
Nor in algorithmic ones.

The question is not:
Who controls everything?
But rather:
Where are points of intervention possible?

The Return of Limitation

Every era eventually discovers its own limits:

- physics discovers energy limits,
- economics discovers resource scarcity,
- computer science discovers complexity limits,
- AI discovers interpretability limits.

The algorithmic age discovers:
The limit of complete prediction.

The Deratification of the Future

When algorithmic esotericism disappears, no empty field remains.
Rather, a more sober realization:

The future is not written by a hidden power.
It arises from:

- interactions,
- decisions,
- systems,
- feedback loops,
- chance.

Not less complex.
But less mystical.

Concluding Observation

"Beyond algorithmic esotericism" does not mean the end of systems.
It means the end of their mythical glorification.

The world remains:

- fast,
- networked,
- data-driven,
- algorithmically shaped.

But it becomes more understandable as soon as one stops treating it as a secret.

The real insight of this book is therefore:
The future is not hidden.
It is distributed.

EPILOGUE – The Spirits We Summoned

What Remains When the Systems Overtake Us – and Yet We Built Them Anyway

"Humans create tools to order the world. And at some point realize that they themselves have become part of the order."

The Last Shadow of the Narrative

Every great technological era leaves a similar trace:
First, a tool emerges.
Then an infrastructure.
Then a system.
Then a dependency.
And at some point, the quiet question:
Do we still have it under control – or has it long been running without us?

The previous chapters of this book have unfolded this development:

- from markets that think,
- to models that decide,
- to systems that generate rules.

Yet in the epilogue, the perspective shifts.
No longer are the systems at the center.

But rather the relationship between human and system.

The Metaphor of Spirits

The expression "the spirits we summoned" is not a warning in the moral sense.
It is a description of a typical dynamic:
Humans create processes that become larger than their original intention.

- fire that was supposed to provide warmth becomes industry,
- money that was supposed to facilitate exchange becomes a global system,
- networks that were supposed to improve communication become infrastructure of power.

And each of these developments initially remains controllable.
Until it no longer is.

The Moment of Irreversibility

There is no clear point at which control is lost.
Instead, there are transitions:

- small automations,

- then scaling,
- then networking,
- then acceleration,
- then dependency.

And at some point, the system is no longer "used."
It is "presupposed."
That is the true turning point.

The New Form of Powerlessness

The classical idea of powerlessness was simple:
One had no access to decisions.

The new form is more subtle:
One is part of the system that decides.

Humans:

- train the models,
- generate the data,
- use the platforms,
- react to the signals.

And at the same time believe they stand outside.
Yet the outside hardly exists anymore.

The Cycle of Self-Reinforcement

The systems described in this book follow a recurring pattern:

1. Data is generated
2. Models are trained
3. Decisions are made
4. Behavior is influenced
5. New behavior generates new data

This cycle is not stable in a static sense.
It is dynamically stable.
It constantly adapts.
And therein lies its strength – and its opacity.

The Quiet Shift of Responsibility

In classical societies, responsibility was localized.
An actor made a decision.
They could be held accountable.

In algorithmic systems, responsibility is distributed:

- developers,
- operators,
- users,
- data suppliers,
- infrastructure,
- market logic.

The more complex the system, the more diffuse the responsibility.
Not because it disappears.
But because it dissolves.

The Normality of the Incomprehensible

One of the most profound changes of the present is not technological.
But cultural:

People are beginning to use systems they no longer fully understand.
This is no longer a state of emergency.
It is everyday life.

- smartphones,
- financial markets,
- AI systems,
- recommendation systems,
- automated decisions.

The world works – even without complete understanding.

The New Invisibility

Earlier power was visible:

- buildings,
- institutions,
- persons,
- symbols.

New power is functional:

- algorithms,
- interfaces,
- data flows,
- models.

It has no face.
No center.
No clear address.

And precisely for that reason, it is often underestimated.

The Question of Human Responsibility

Despite all automation, one fact remains:
Every one of these systems was created by humans.
Not in the sense of direct control.
But in the sense of structural design.

Humans defined:

- goals,

- optimization functions,
- data sources,
- architectural decisions.

The spirits are therefore not foreign.
They are human-generated – and then became autonomous.

The Ambivalence of Progress

Technological progress is never unequivocal:
It simultaneously increases:

- freedom and dependency,
- efficiency and fragility,
- knowledge and overwhelm,
- control and complexity.

The systems of this book are not a mistake.
They are a consequence.

The Return of the Question of Meaning

When systems increasingly operate autonomously, the central question shifts:
No longer only:
How does it work?

But rather:
What does it exist for?

Because a system can function perfectly
and still be socially problematic
if its goal no longer aligns with human values.

The Final Responsibility

At the end of all algorithmic structures, a simple, uncomfortable truth remains:
There are no "external" systems.
Only systems that humans built – and continue to build.

Even if no one has an overview anymore,
responsibility remains distributed among those
who continue to change the architecture.

The Possibility of Recapture

History is not linear.
Every complex development also contains counter-movements:

- regulation,
- transparency initiatives,
- open-source movements,

•democratic control,
•technological education.

These forces are not romantic.
They are structurally necessary.
Because every stable civilization needs feedback with its own system.

The True Meaning of the "Spirits"

The spirits we summoned are not foreign entities.
They are:

•accelerated processes,
•scaled decisions,
•automated logics,
•networked systems.

They do not act against us.
But also not automatically for us.
They follow the goals we inscribed in them – often indirectly, often historically grown, often unconsciously.

Concluding Observation

The epilogue of this book is not an end in the classical sense.

It is a return.
To the opening question:

Who controls the invisible forces that shape global systems?

The answer is less dramatic than the metaphors suggest – and at the same time more demanding:
Not one instance controls them.
But many levels of decisions that condense into structures over time.

The real challenge therefore does not lie in "defeating" these systems.
But in understanding, shaping, and limiting what we ourselves have created.

The spirits we summoned did not come to replace us.
They came to show us how deeply we already live within our own systems.

References to Publications

The Age of AI

The Age of AI: And Our Human Future is a 2021 nonfiction book about the societal and geopolitical implications of artificial intelligence, co-authored by Henry A. Kissinger, Eric Schmidt, and Daniel Huttenlocher. It blends foreign policy, industry, and academic perspectives to argue that AI is transforming how knowledge is created and how power is organized.

Key Facts

- Full title: *The Age of AI: And Our Human Future*
- Authors: Henry A. Kissinger, Eric Schmidt, Daniel Huttenlocher
- Publication year: 2021 (Little, Brown and Company)
- Length: Approximately 270–290 pages, depending on edition
- Main theme: How AI reshapes knowledge, power, and international order

Background and Authorship

The book brings together three distinct backgrounds: Kissinger as a veteran diplomat and strategist, Schmidt as former CEO of Google, and Huttenlocher as a computer scientist and academic leader. Their collaboration grew out of shared concerns that AI's rise is changing human affairs as profoundly as the printing press or the scientific revolution – but faster and with less public understanding.

Core Themes and Arguments

The book argues that AI systems don't just process information; they generate novel patterns, predictions, and strategies that humans might not be able to fully retrace or explain. This undermines traditional ideas of causality, expertise, and responsibility. The authors explore how this shift could affect diplomacy, military strategy, economic competition, and domestic politics, and they call for new conceptual frameworks and institutions to manage AI's power.

Style, Structure, and Reception

The text is essayistic and reflective rather than technical, aiming at policymakers and general readers rather than engineers. Reviewers note that it offers a broad, high-level roadmap and powerful metaphors, but can be light on technical detail and empirical rigor; some critics argue it contributes to "AI hype" by emphasizing AI's transformative power without always carefully delineating current limitations.

Place in the AI Discourse

The Age of AI sits alongside other big-picture works on AI and society, influencing debates on AI governance, national security, and ethics. The authors have extended its arguments in op-eds and policy discussions, framing AI as a strategic technology that demands sustained public, academic, and governmental engagement.

Architects of Intelligence

Architects of Intelligence: The Truth About AI from the People Building It is a 2018 nonfiction book by futurist and author Martin Ford. It presents extended interviews with 23 leading figures in artificial intelligence about the future of AI, its technical trajectory, and its social, economic, and ethical implications.

Key Facts

- Author: Martin Ford
- Publication year: 2018
- Publisher: Packt Publishing
- Form: Interview-style nonfiction, approximately 550 pages
- Subject: Future of artificial intelligence and its impact on work, economy, and society

Content and Structure

The book is organized as a series of in-depth, one-to-one interviews with prominent researchers and entrepreneurs in AI. Interviewees include figures such as Demis Hassabis, Geoffrey Hinton, Yann LeCun, Yoshua Bengio, Fei-Fei Li, Nick Bostrom, Andrew Ng, and others.

Each chapter centers on one expert's perspective, covering topics such as deep learning, reinforcement learning, robotics, and prospects for artificial general intelligence (AGI). The conversations explore both technical directions and broader questions about timelines, opportunities, and systemic risks.

Themes and Focus

A central theme is how AI will transform labor markets and the global economy. Ford repeatedly raises issues like technological unemployment, inequality, and possible policy responses, including social safety nets and new economic models. Interviewees often disagree on timelines and severity of disruption, giving a spectrum of expert opinion rather than a single forecast.

Another major focus is AI safety and ethics: alignment problems, autonomous weapons, bias in machine-learning systems, and governance of powerful AI technologies. Several interviews consider paths toward human-level or superhuman AI and debate whether these advances are near-term, long-term, or even desirable.

Reception and Significance

Architects of Intelligence has been noted as providing a "snapshot" of elite AI opinion around the late-2010s deep-learning boom. Commentators have highlighted it as a useful resource for understanding how leading practitioners themselves think about impact, timelines, and uncertainty in AI's development.

Power and Surveillance

The Age of Surveillance Capitalism

The Age of Surveillance Capitalism: The Fight for a Human Future at the New Frontier of Power is a 2019 nonfiction book by scholar Shoshana Zuboff. It examines how major technology companies exploit personal data to shape behavior and generate profit. The work has been widely discussed for its critical analysis of digital-era capitalism and its social consequences.

Key Facts

- Author: Shoshana Zuboff
- Published: 2019 (PublicAffairs)
- Genre: Nonfiction, technology, political economy
- Main focus: Corporate use of personal data for behavioral prediction
- Length: Approximately 700 pages

Concept and Argument

Zuboff introduces the term *surveillance capitalism* to describe an economic system in which companies such as Google, Facebook, and others claim private human experience as raw material for data extraction. This data is processed into predictive products sold to advertisers and other entities seeking to forecast and influence user behavior. Zuboff argues this dynamic marks a new phase of capitalism that threatens autonomy and democracy.

Historical Context

The book situates surveillance capitalism in the wake of the early internet's commercialization and the 2000s rise of data-driven business models. It traces a lineage from industrial capitalism's control over nature to digital capitalism's control over human behavior. Zuboff contrasts this new form of power with earlier notions of information capitalism that were more participatory and transparent.

Reception and Influence

The Age of Surveillance Capitalism received critical acclaim for its depth and scope, often compared to classic social critiques of industrial capitalism. It has influenced debates in technology policy, privacy law, and digital ethics, prompting renewed discussion of data rights and platform regulation. Critics note its dense style but recognize it as a foundational text for understanding contemporary digital power structures.

Platform Capitalism

Platform Capitalism is a 2016 book by political economist Nick Srnicek. It analyzes how digital platforms – such as those run by Google, Amazon, and Uber – reshape capitalism by creating new forms of value extraction and market dominance through data control and network effects.

Key Facts

- Author: Nick Srnicek
- Published: 2016
- Publisher: Polity Press

- Genre: Political economy, technology studies
- Main focus: Economic logic of digital platforms

Background and Context

The book situates itself in debates about post-industrial capitalism and the rise of the digital economy. Srnicek argues that following the 2008 financial crisis, corporations sought new profit models, leading to the expansion of data-driven business structures known as platforms. This shift represents a new stage of capitalist development rather than a departure from it.

Core Arguments

Srnicek classifies platforms into categories – advertising, cloud, industrial, product, and lean platforms – to explain how each extracts and monetizes data. He contends that these firms benefit from network effects, leading to monopolistic or oligopolistic market outcomes. Data becomes the central commodity, enabling predictive analytics and targeted services that reinforce corporate power.

Reception and Influence

The book has been widely discussed in academic and policy circles for providing a clear theoretical framework to understand companies like Facebook and Uber. Scholars of digital labor, critical technology studies, and political economy often use it as a foundational text to describe "platform capitalism" as a distinct economic form.

Legacy and Relevance

Platform Capitalism remains influential in discussions of digital regulation, surveillance, and automation. It continues to inform analyses of how technological infrastructures shape work, inequality, and global competition in the twenty-first century.

Financial Systems

Flash Boys

Flash Boys: A Wall Street Revolt is a nonfiction book by Michael Lewis, published in 2014. It investigates the rise of high-frequency trading (HFT) in U.S. equity markets and argues that advanced technology allowed certain firms to gain unfair advantages. The work became a bestseller for its accessible exposé of modern market structure.

Key Facts

- Author: Michael Lewis
- Published: 2014

•Publisher: W. W. Norton & Company
•Subject: High-frequency trading and market fairness
•Genre: Investigative finance nonfiction

Background and Context

Michael Lewis, known for works such as *The Big Short* and *Moneyball*, turned his attention to financial markets' technological transformation following the 2008 crisis. *Flash Boys* traces how fragmented exchanges, fiber-optic cables, and algorithmic strategies altered equity trading and eroded investor trust in market transparency.

Synopsis

The narrative centers on Brad Katsuyama, a trader at Royal Bank of Canada, who discovers that his orders are consistently disadvantaged by faster traders. He and his team uncover how milliseconds of latency enable HFT firms to "front-run" trades. Their response is creating the Investors Exchange (IEX), designed to neutralize speed advantages through a "speed bump" that delays orders by microseconds.

Impact and Reception

The book reignited debate about market fairness and the role of technology in finance. It spurred congressional hearings and regulatory scrutiny of

HFT practices. Critics from the trading community argued Lewis overstated the harm, while supporters praised the book's clarity in exposing opaque systems. It reached the top of *The New York Times* bestseller list and influenced public perception of modern finance.

Legacy

Flash Boys remains a key text in discussions of financial ethics, market design, and algorithmic trading. It helped elevate Katsuyama and IEX as reform advocates and solidified Lewis's reputation as a leading chronicler of systemic change in complex industries.

Dark Pools

Dark Pools: The Rise of the Machine Traders and the Rigging of the U.S. Stock Market is a 2012 nonfiction book by financial journalist Scott Patterson. It investigates the evolution of high-frequency and algorithmic trading and their impact on modern financial markets. The book gained attention for its detailed narrative on how technology reshaped Wall Street's trading infrastructure.

Key Facts

- Author: Scott Patterson
- Published: 2012
- Genre: Nonfiction, finance
- Publisher: Crown Business
- Subject: High-frequency trading and market structure

Background and Premise

Patterson, a reporter for *The Wall Street Journal*, traces the history of electronic trading from its early development in the 1990s through the 2000s. He explores how a small group of programmers and quantitative analysts built algorithmic systems that began to dominate trading volumes. The book's title refers to "dark pools," private exchanges or forums for trading securities outside public stock markets.

Content and Themes

Dark Pools examines the technological and ethical consequences of the shift from human to machine-driven trading. It details how high-frequency traders exploited millisecond advantages and how opaque trading venues fragmented market transparency. Patterson frames this as both an innovation story and a cautionary tale about systemic risk and fairness in capital markets.

Reception and Influence

The book was praised for making complex financial systems accessible to general readers while maintaining journalistic rigor. Critics compared it to *Flash Boys* by Michael Lewis, which appeared later and explored similar territory. *Dark Pools* influenced public and regulatory debates over market structure and remains a reference point in discussions about financial automation and ethics.

Systems Theory

Social Systems

Social Systems (*Soziale Systeme*) is a 1984 book by German sociologist Niklas Luhmann. It is one of his most influential works, outlining a general theory of social systems that shaped late 20th-century sociology. The book presents a radical reinterpretation of society through systems theory and cybernetics, emphasizing communication rather than action as the core of social life.

Key Facts

- Author: Niklas Luhmann
- Original publication: 1984 (Suhrkamp Verlag, Frankfurt am Main)

•Language: German
•English translation: *Social Systems* (1995, translated by John Bednarz Jr. and Dirk Baecker)
•Discipline: Sociology / Systems theory

Theoretical Background

Luhmann developed *Social Systems* as part of his broader project to apply autopoietic systems theory, originally derived from biology, to the social world. He built on ideas from Talcott Parsons, Humberto Maturana, and Francisco Varela to describe society as a self-producing network of communications, distinct from individuals or psychological systems.

Core Concepts

The book argues that social systems are autopoietic – they reproduce themselves through communication. Communication, not individual consciousness or action, is the unit of analysis. Luhmann defines several subsystems (e.g., law, politics, economy) that operate via their own binary codes and maintain operational closure while being cognitively open to their environment.

Influence and Reception

Social Systems marked a turning point in systems theory and European sociology, influencing fields such as organization theory, legal studies, and media theory. Though often considered difficult and abstract, it positioned Luhmann as a major figure in contemporary social theory and contributed to the development of second-order cybernetics.

Legacy

The ideas from *Social Systems* continued in Luhmann's later works, notably *Die Gesellschaft der Gesellschaft* (1997). Its English translation broadened its international impact, integrating systems theory into sociological and philosophical debates beyond German-speaking countries.

The Protestant Ethic and the Spirit of Capitalism

The Protestant Ethic and the Spirit of Capitalism (*Die protestantische Ethik und der Geist des Kapitalismus*) is a sociological work by Max Weber, first published in 1904–1905. It examines how Protestant religious values – particularly those of Calvinism – helped shape the cultural conditions that fostered the rise of modern capitalism in Western Europe.

Key Facts

- Author: Max Weber
- First publication: 1904–1905 (revised 1920)
- Language: German
- Subject: Sociology, economics, religion
- Core theme: Link between Protestant ethics and capitalist spirit

Background and Purpose

Weber wrote the book as part of a broader inquiry into the relationship between religion and economic behavior. He challenged purely materialist explanations of capitalism, arguing that cultural and spiritual factors also played a decisive role. His analysis built on earlier work in sociology and economics but introduced a distinctive focus on moral motivation.

Main Argument

Weber proposed that aspects of Protestantism – especially the Calvinist idea of a "calling" and belief in predestination – encouraged disciplined, rational labor and the reinvestment of profits rather than lavish consumption. Over time, this ethos fostered a "spirit" conducive to capitalist enterprise and bureaucratic organization, even after its religious origins had waned.

Influence and Reception

The work is a foundational text in the sociology of religion and economic sociology. It influenced later thinkers such as Talcott Parsons and shaped debates on modernization and secularization. Though some historians have questioned Weber's causal claims, his concept of the "Protestant ethic" remains a key analytical tool in understanding Western capitalism's cultural roots.

Legacy

Today, *The Protestant Ethic and the Spirit of Capitalism* continues to inform studies in sociology, economics, and cultural history. It exemplifies Weber's broader project of analyzing the rationalization of Western society and the tensions between economic progress and spiritual meaning.

Philosophy of Technology

The Question Concerning Technology

The Question Concerning Technology (*Die Frage nach der Technik*) is a 1954 essay by German philosopher Martin Heidegger. It examines the essence of modern technology beyond its instrumental use, arguing that technology shapes how humans reveal and relate to the world. The essay remains one of Heidegger's most influential and widely studied works in 20th-century philosophy.

Key Facts

- Author: Martin Heidegger
- First publication: 1954 (lecture delivered in 1953)
- Original language: German
- Central concept: *Gestell* ("enframing")
- Collected in: *Vorträge und Aufsätze* (1954)

Philosophical Background

Heidegger developed this essay during his later period, when he shifted from existential analysis toward questions of Being (*Sein*). Drawing on earlier work such as *Being and Time* (*Sein und Zeit*), he sought to explore how technological thinking reveals – or conceals – the essence of Being. The essay formed part of a series of lectures connecting metaphysics, art, and modernity.

Core Argument

Heidegger distinguishes between technology as a tool (instrumental) and as a mode of revealing (ontological). Modern technology, he claims, "enframes" (*Gestell*) the world, ordering it as a "standing-reserve" (*Bestand*) of resources available for exploitation. This enframing conceals alternative ways of revealing truth, thereby endangering a more poetic or contemplative relation to Being.

Influence and Interpretation

The Question Concerning Technology deeply influenced continental philosophy, science and technology studies, and environmental thought. Thinkers such as Jacques Ellul, Herbert Marcuse, and later post-phenomenologists expanded or critiqued Heidegger's account. The essay continues to shape debates on technological determinism, ethics, and ecological responsibility.

Legacy

Today, *The Question Concerning Technology* is a cornerstone text in philosophy of technology and media studies. Its vocabulary – especially *Gestell* and *Bestand* – has become standard for analyzing how technology structures perception, culture, and power in the modern world.